MW01224273

each small step

◆

breaking the chains of abuse and addiction

an anthology of writing

by and for women who are

childhood sexual abuse survivors

and have been affected by chemical dependency

The Staff and Board of the Women's Post Treatment Centre wish to acknowledge and thank Tanya Lester, Heidi Eigenkind and Marilyn Mac-Kinnon for their dedication and commitment. It is doubtful that this book would have been completed without the efforts of Tanya and Heidi, who did the majority of the work leading up to the first draft of the manuscript. To Marilyn, who assembled, designed and edited a vast amount of material to produce the final manuscript, we want to offer our special thanks and admiration for her skill and perseverance. But, most of all, we would like to thank all the women who took the risk of contributing their very private and painful feelings and memories in the hope that they would help others to follow the path towards healing.

With thanks to the Canada Council and to the Department of National Health and Welfare for their generous support.

gynergy books
P.O. Box 2023
Charlottetown
Prince Edward Island
Canada C1A 7N7

Cover Artwork: *Flying Blue* by Kathleen Knowling
Cover & Book Design: Catherine Matthews
Printed & Bound in Canada by: Hignell Printing Ltd.

Canadian Cataloguing in Publication Data
Main entry under title:
Each small step
ISBN 0-921881-17-7
1. Incest victims. 2. Adult child sexual abuse victims. 3. Substance abuse — Patients — Manitoba — Biography. 4. Women — Substance abuse.
I. MacKinnon, Marilyn, 1951-
RC569.5.C55E32 1991   362.8   C91-097669-4

I am shattering all the silence.
I am going to make noise. I want
to speak. I want to make choices and
to feel free. Free from restrictions,
from hiding. I don't want to hide
anymore. I want to be me.

—K.G.

♦

"I am the only daughter of Air Force parents and have three younger brothers. My voice as a child was silent. I spoke through writing and art. I continue to do so."

— K.G.

contents

introduction

Marilyn MacKinnon

*T*his book is for survivors of childhood sexual abuse and chemical addiction, and all those interested in better understanding the connection between these two afflictions in women's lives. It began five years ago as a project of the Women's Post Treatment Centre (WPTC) in Winnipeg to give a public voice to the women who have come to this agency seeking help in coping with the terrible memories that sobriety unleashed.

For the most part, the small percentage of the women who came to the WPTC and were not drug or alcohol dependent, come from alcoholic families. For the handful who do not fit one or both of these categories, life had become unbearable by the time they arrived at the WPTC. Usually these women were in their 30s and 40s. Women older and younger than this are beginning to come forward as well—evidence of the cumulative impact of the women's movement, the movement against domestic violence and, in particular, the media coverage and publications on childhood sexual abuse of the last eight-or-so years.

This book is charged with emotional intensity. With a few exceptions, the writings are by survivors of this two-pronged trauma. Whether you, the reader, are a survivor or not, we offer the same caution in approaching this text. Use the table of contents to pick out what you want to address at the moment. Set a time limit, then leave the book for a few days and see how you feel. If, at any time, the material is unleashing an avalanche of feelings, put it aside. Call a friend or counsellor. Even if you have read extensively in this area, this book cannot help but engender strong feelings of anger and grief.

For these reasons there are important questions that you should ask yourself every time you pick up this book: "Why am I reading this? What am I looking for?" We asked similar questions in compiling and editing this book. I'd like to list the answers, for they shaped the book you are now holding.

◆

First, *Each Small Step* exists to offer regional proof that widespread childhood sexual abuse exists, and that addiction is a common factor in homes and situations where sexual abuse occurs, and in the aftermath of the abuse. Most of these stories are from women in the Province of Manitoba. They represent only a fraction of the women who are known to be seeking help in dealing with childhood sexual abuse.

Over fifty percent of women alcoholics report that they were sexually abused as children. This book also seeks to present the stories behind this statistic.

If these were the only answers to the question, "What is this book for?", this book would be full of horror stories and anger. To be sure, the horror and its rightful response, anger, are here. But we felt it was equally important to chart the journey to healing which many women are navigating with incredible courage, intelligence and wisdom.

The writers in this anthology wanted to share their outrage, which they hope will be echoed in the public's response. They also wanted to share their developing sense of pride and dignity.

The writers also wished to share, with their sister survivors, their courage, their love, and information about the things that have helped them along the way.

◆

These women are wrestling with two of the most daunting traumas imaginable. It is difficult enough to be a woman recovering from alcoholism or drug addiction. Although Alcoholics Anonymous, the most well-known and sucessful sobriety program in existence, has helped millions of women and men, it has involved only a fraction of alcoholics, and an even smaller percentage of women alcoholics (3%).

Fifteen years ago, Jean Kirkpatrick, author of *Turnabout, New Help for the Woman Alcoholic* started Women for Sobriety, an organization in which she charted her steps to sobriety in order to help other women recover. Although many women in this book have achieved sobriety through A.A., some have found it limited in its helpfulness. Apparently they, like Jean Kirkpatrick, find they need a more affirming, gentler, more "female" approach to recovering from addiction. This echoes many women's problems with organized religion—its hierarchies and male, or father, metaphors for God. In fact many women, as well as men, who have been abused as children have problems with parental metaphors of any kind—at least until significant healing has taken place.

Each Small Step does not advocate any sobriety program in particular, nor any particular therapeutic model for recovery from childhood sexual abuse. The editors who have worked on this book have attempted to hear everything these survivors have reported. We believe, as they do, that in telling all of their story as they are ready and able to at a given time, healing is facilitated. We ask the readers to give them the same attention, and to put the book aside when this is not possible.

Blaming the victim shows an inability to cope with the truth, and it is a failure that does the victim further harm. All the contributors in this book say that the very hardest thing they suffered was to be blamed and silenced. They also say the greatest safety for them is in being heard and believed.

The aim of this book, then, is that the survivors be heard and believed. For survivors to become whole and healthy, they are asking our communities and organizations to respond in a way that civilized states have usually failed to do. They are asking us to listen, to believe, and to support them and the programs that help them heal.

It is easy to lose perspective in the great raging sorrow that is the subject of this book. Pacing is important if individual survivors, and our communities and society at large, are to heal.

For readers who are not survivors it is instructive to remember that survivors usually have great difficulty accessing their memories, and even when they do, they have recurring difficulty in believing them. Perpetrators also have memory problems about abuse, and alcohol is often an aid in this. As a society we have also found rich and varied ways to forget.

Alice Miller, a former psychoanalyst and author of numerous books on childhood abuse and repression, looks back almost one hundred years for a very instructive example. "Freud," she writes in *Banished Knowledge* (1990), "originally discovered, in the treatments partially conducted under hypnosis, that all his patients, both male and female, had been abused children and recounted their histories in the language of symptoms. After reporting his discovery in psychiatric circles, he found himself completely shunned because none of his fellow psychiatrists were prepared to share the findings with him. Freud could not bear the isolation for long. A few months later, in 1897, he described his patient's reports as sheer fantasies attributable to their intellectual wishes. Humanity's briefly disturbed sleep could now be resumed."

Most likely, the widespread failure to remember is the result of our society's inability to listen. It is in telling our stories that we ourselves first hear them. We shape our stories, and our lives, in accordance with our audience's willingness and ability to hear.

Each Small Step is a testament to the struggle to heal—from both childhood sexual abuse and addiction. But at its core are lessons that affect all of our society, lessons about childhood, parenting, addiction, and healing. In *For Your Own Good, Hidden Cruelty in Child Rearing and the Roots of Violence* (1983), Alice Miller writes, "With the knowledge of one's own history ... blindness is no longer required as a protection from fear. Someone who has faced facts need no longer fear reality or flee from it."

Addiction grows out of flight and fear. Barbara Ball, co-founder of the WPTC, which pioneered post-addiction treatment for survivors of childhood sexual abuse in Canada, says, "We knew when we started that it was not lack of motivation that caused women to go back to behaviour that was labelled self-destructive or insane. They were going back to survive—either to feel the feelings and not feel dead inside, or to numb the pain."

The writers in this book report that they retrieve pieces of themselves as they remember their abuse and that this remembering is episodic. But they also report that they are in jeopardy of losing *all* of themselves while they are remembering. This process is akin to childbirth, where the risk of death hovers even as the baby is born.

This is where knowledgeable support comes in. Barbara Ball's article on the struggle to have that need recognized and start the WPTC follows this introduction. And her instructive article about the "disease model" of addiction, its virtues and its limitations, especially for women, is in the section of the book called "Reaching Out: Becoming Whole."

When the WPTC was formed in the mid 1980s, Barbara Ball and her colleagues searched for information about the connection between childhood sexual abuse and chemical dependency. That search led them to psychologist Sue Evans and her associates, who were already working in this field in Minneapolis, Minnesota.

As we, the editors and compilers, searched for ways to present this connection in a book of writing by survivors, some of Sue Evans' academic writing was pulled out. After reading pieces by survivors, and interviewing many more, I found that Sue's writings provided a powerful connection to what they were relating. Especially relevant was a 1984 article entitled, "Shame, Boundaries and Dissociation in Chemically Dependent, Abusive and Incestuous Families."

It seemed natural to ask Sue Evans to contribute an overview piece for *Each Small Step*. She agreed, and I interviewed her when she arrived in Winnipeg for a conference on chemical dependency. That interview, which is divided into parts which precede each section in the book, is meant to enhance and provide perspective for the survivor-authored pieces which are the raison d'être for *Each Small Step*.

Although the survivors assert that the basis of their healing is in "feeling the feelings" associated with their experiences of abuse, and Sue Evans' writing echoes that approach to healing, it is also true that an intellectual framework can provide signposts for the difficult journey. For instance, the "boundary violation chart" which follows the first part of the interview with Sue, is helpful in understanding the various kinds of invasions of personal boundaries that damage self-esteem.

In her interview, Sue Evans talks about "victims." At the WPTC, and in the women's community, people who have lived through experiences of childhood sexual abuse are *survivors*, not victims. Indeed, their very existence, the fact that they are not dead, not insane, have families of their own, hold jobs and lead busy, productive lives, heralds them as courageous survivors.

It is in therapy, in self-help groups, individually in their writing, drawing and body work, and in their closest relationships, that survivors unravel the "victim" issues that haunt them. And it is from within that shadow that Sue Evans, as a helper and psychologist, writes.

Obviously, for most of these writers there was very little parenting in their lives. Miraculously, most eagerly accepted what little they were offered. Even more stunning is the amount of parenting these women gave their parents and/or abusers, providing love, emotional support, domestic labour—all the while being used for sexual gratification, as an outlet for rage, and to satisfy the need to control and overpower a vulnerable and innocent being.

The contributors to *Each Small Step* write frequently of the little girl inside them—long abandoned, waiting patiently to be found again. This inner child, care-giver extraordinaire, also has a fine-tuned sense of justice—one that incorporates a morality of concern, and connection to other people, with a sense of fairness. It is women with this child finally embraced and intact who are starting to take their abusers to court for damages.

As the young Winnipeg woman, who received $170,000 in damages after suing her father for ten years of sexual abuse, said to reporters, "It means to me that people and society are starting to take a stand and say this isn't allowed."

These kind of judicial decisions and settlements, along with counselling and support, will go some distance towards altering the social equation in which the victim pays and the abuser doesn't.

That these women had their childhood stolen goes without saying. That they lost their voice is clear, and they write here to regain it. They also write of learning and experiencing in adult life what childhood is, what play and fun are, and what sex is, and isn't. They write of re-entering their lost bodies, finding an untapped reservoir of laughter, learning of their intelligence, feeling the sun shine on their skin. Slowly they realize what courageous human beings they are. And usually, lighting every step of the way, is a bright torch of anger.

◆

I have referred countless times in this introduction to "we." By this I mean the working group that hired and supported me and worked so hard in the process of compiling *Each Small Step*. I would like to thank them—Barbara Ball, Sheila Konyk, Laura Donatelli, Hazel Blennerhassett and Darlene Gibson—for their warmth, insight and intelligence, and their tireless commitment to the survivors. I would also like to thank all the contributors, many of whom I met only over the phone, for their trust and uncommon honesty.

I came to this project from a background in writing and editing, and a dusty old degree, for which I had studied community development and self-help groups. But my strongest connection to this project began through a friend who, several years after we had become pals, started to remember being sexually abused as a little girl. She is a great friend and a fine woman. I hope this book does her, and all the marvellous contributors, justice.

— Marilyn MacKinnon

—D.C.

the women's
post treatment centre

◆

"I am a single native parent from northern Manitoba. I have three beautiful children. I work as a management trainee for the government. One of my favourite pastimes is sketching. Basically I am an optimist. I believe that all things are possible."

— D.C.

why a women's post treatment centre?

Barbara Ball

*T*he Women's Post Treatment Centre is one attempt to combat denial of the sexual abuse of children and the damage it does. It is also an attempt to assist the many women who are struggling to come to terms with childhood victimization and one of its many aftermaths—chemical dependency.

We believe that if one organizational mandate links the two issues, denial will be lessened and services will become more relevant.

In the early 1980s, women's problems of dependence on alcohol and drugs were not being viewed or understood in the light of childhood experiences of victimization—sexual, emotional and physical. Chemical dependency was understood as a "disease" and *only* a disease. This definition led to looking for a solution within a woman's psychology and physiology without reference to a woman's current and past experience and how she was perceiving and interpreting it. Because of this mindset, what "addicted" women were beginning to describe about abuse experiences (to those who would listen) was being largely ignored by policy makers and in treatment programs.

Women's experience challenged the prevailing viewpoint. What did this mean in terms of treatment? It meant that Mary (age twenty-nine) could not talk about her nightmares and flashbacks of childhood sexual abuse experiences because she was in an "addiction treatment program" *not* a program to treat sexual abuse. After three weeks, she went back to drinking in order to feel more sane. It meant that Janet (age sixty)—and in addiction treatment for the third time—was (again) not "able to open up to her counsellor" and therefore seen as "resistant" or "not ready." (No one had ever described "sexual abuse" to her or asked her if she needed to talk about it. She did not see herself as a victim of sexual abuse because her grandfather "never actually penetrated" her.) If someone had asked her the right questions, giving her permission to talk, she would have broken her silence. She might have begun to feel like less of a "failure," realizing that her drinking was related directly to surviving a life of victimization, a role her grandfather had trained her in from age five when he began sexually abusing her.

It meant that Renata, who had been sexually abused by eleven different male relatives, might also have seen that her use of alcohol which began at age eight, was the only course of action open to her then. There was no caring capable adult in her world. In order to stop using alcohol as an adult, she would need time to learn some other ways to survive. While she was being taught in treatment about the phases and stages of "her disease," she was feeling guilty and confused. Inside herself she knew that without drinking she would have committed suicide long ago. No one was acknowledging this. Deep down, she knew she would not be able to stay off alcohol. She could not say this out loud. It would not have been "okay."

It meant that Renata and Mary and Janet were not being helped to see their behaviour with drinking and drugs as something sane and rational—something that had helped them survive in an insane, unsafe and abusive world in which they had no nurturing or protection and in which they were being exploited in a way that was morally and criminally wrong.

We were just not making these connections in our chemical addiction programs, yet woman after woman (if asked), disclosed abuse. Many readily related their purpose in using alcohol and drugs as one of coping with feelings and memories of childhood and adolescence. Codeine pills or syrup, tranquilizers, a drink, a toke, or street drugs—the choice of drug differed but the function was similar. Victimization was the common denominator.

There were other women too. Those who had grown up in homes with a parent chronically abusing chemicals. Some of these women avoided alcohol or drugs; others were using hazardously. They too disclosed problems related to abuse and addiction. The chance of being abused in an "alcoholic" family is much greater.

As helpers, some of us shared our growing feelings of frustration at not having the time and mandate to open the "can of worms" when women disclosed their abuse, and, at the same time, having no other resource for treatment. Encouraging disclosure would just make it worse because the abuse couldn't be properly worked through. Many helpers survived by ignoring these abuse issues and focusing on "the disease of chemical dependency."

The Women's Post Treatment Centre began when some of us in counselling roles kept talking about the common denominator of sexual abuse. We met others at workshops about sexual abuse, and through other agencies working with women. We felt angry that no one was listening to the women who were our clients. We felt angry about the widespread denial of women's abuse experiences. We felt frustrated with the concept of "disease." As the only accepted concept, it was part of the wall of societal denial that hid childhood sexual abuse.

We knew that women were not going back to behaviour that was labelled "self-destructive" or "insane" because they were unmotivated. They were doing this to survive; sometimes because they lacked other ways to kill the overwhelming feelings, and other times to "feel some feelings," to dispel for a while "the numbness," and sense of being "dead" inside.

Some women got together, in mid-1984, encouraged by a United Church minister, our families and supportive friends. We formed a small steering committee—which grew from three to six, and then to eight. We worked for months researching and developing a funding proposal in consultation with a senior staff person at the Alcoholism Foundation. We felt increasingly confident. Our ideas made sense, especially to the many women we consulted who had been affected by addiction and childhood sexual abuse.

We were confident our proposal would be accepted and "sponsored" by the Alcoholism Foundation, making us eligible to receive funding to start a "demonstration project."

The phone call came after their Board meeting in early 1985. Our proposal requesting sponsorship had been rejected. It did not fall closely enough within the Foundation's mandate.

In fact, no agency focused on the trauma of childhood sexual abuse. It fell between the cracks. Yet, to us, it was related to chemical dependency as well as to mental health, physical health, justice and family welfare. Between twenty-five and fifty percent of all women have experienced some form of childhood sexual abuse. Of women seeking addiction treatment, the percentages we found were close to ninety percent. Someone had to begin to acknowledge this!

At this point, we had come to a dead end. We faced the discouraging reality that, with no parent body, we were not eligible to receive the available funding. In a series of meetings, we talked about abandoning our project. We were eight dejected women nearly ready to give up—but still sharing our anger about the injustice of the denial, and chagrined by our naivety about the system.

Then someone suggested the Salvation Army. "I have a contact there! Let's approach them—one more try before we quit."

That provided our opportunity. The Army-Harbour Light Corps shared our concern and offered what they could: one fourth-floor room in Baldwin House, a phone and, most important, their official sponsorship. They also provided one more member for our steering committee. We became a congenial group of nine women.

With one position, job-shared by two of us, we began offering "post addiction treatment" counselling to women who needed to work on the issue of childhood sexual abuse. As staff, we worked on a slim budget and did our correspondence at night because we had no typewriter or funds for clerical support. Steering committee members pitched in, doing financial reports for us and helping to plan ongoing fund raising. We lobbied, we spoke to groups and government. Our space grew to two rooms.

We persuaded the telephone company to add several feet to our telephone cord, so we could pass our telephone back and forth under the swinging door that separated our two small rooms. At the end of the first year, we had secured enough funding to create three part-time jobs and we increased our staff to three, hiring the social work student who had worked with us for much of the first year.

Through this time, we saw how motivated those women affected by abuse and chemical dependency really were. They came from all kinds of diverse backgrounds—trekking up four dingy, noisy flights of stairs, through a spartan and overcrowded hostel for women and their children. They followed our hand-lettered signs reading "Women's Post Treatment" ... "keep following these arrows" ... "three more flights" ... "two more flights" ... "almost there" ... They kept arriving for appointments, proving over and over again that our perception of the need and our approach to women was correct. The silence about women's experiences was being broken again and again as women welcomed the opportunity to speak and to find within themselves answers for their own lives.

We began leading small groups, to help women break their isolation and identify with others. Some of those women have written for this book. They relate their own sense of that time best.

These first steps felt big but in reality they were small and there were many more to be taken.

We have made much progress and now have five staff. However our future is at risk. We need more funding to maintain our current levels of service. We have a huge waiting list of women needing our help who will wait many months before we can begin counselling.

In order to develop greater financial support we need more widespread societal understanding of the extent of childhood sexual abuse and its impact on the lives of adults. Our experience at the WPTC has convinced us that developing the political will to recognize and meet the needs of these women is a priority if we are to create a more healthy, less violent society.

— K.G.

childhood

under siege

interview with Sue Evans

Sue Evans is a psychologist who works with chemically dependent sexual abuse survivors in Minneapolis, Minnesota. She has worked in this field for fourteen years and is well respected as an author and speaker in both Canada and the United States.

I interviewed Sue over coffee in her hotel after she had already put in a long day speaking at a workshop on "Current Issues in Chemical Dependency" in Winnipeg.

—Marilyn MacKinnon

Part One

Q. How did you start working in the treatment of chemically dependent women?

A. I started as a mental health practitioner about fourteen years ago. It was through Chrysalis that I had my first job out of college. We got some funding to start one of the first women's chemical dependency treatment programs. I spent about six months working with the director, as her assistant, going out and researching what works for women and what doesn't work for women in existing treatment programs and helping the staff to really come up with some plan on how we would do it differently.

Q. Can you remember when childhood sexual abuse first came up in your work with chemically dependent women?

A. From the beginning there were a couple of women on staff who were very powerful advocates for looking at that. They did a wonderful job of making the abuse section a very strong part of the recovery program. I don't think any of us argued with the idea. Anyone who was working with these women at all knew the necessity for it. Sue Schaffer and I worked a lot in the sexuality section, with women who had been sexually abused by people outside the family system.

21

We also worked on sexual enhancement. Ways to counter the female socialization, the woman-hating that we all carry around in our sexuality. Besides having a caseload, we all had a section. So the connection between alcoholism and abuse was always apparent.

Q. If you were to look at chemical dependency and sexual abuse of children from a distance, so we can get a handle on it intellectually, what is the connection?

A. There are a number of ways that they overlap. In a broad sense, people use chemicals in order to medicate the feelings around the abuse of children, whether it be physical abuse or incest or abuse by a stranger. And if they are victims of abuse there is a lot of shame—what did I do wrong, what is the matter with me, why did he pick me or why did she pick me? There is a lot of anguish in just feeling the feelings of the abuse and people medicate the feelings away, or they try to. And eventually the addictive nature of the drug takes over. People also tend to medicate their urges of wanting to abuse kids. Certainly you can be a child abuser and not be an alcoholic. But alcohol is also used to release inhibitions, and some abusers do a lot of things after a couple of drinks that they wouldn't do sober.

Underlying that, I think there are similarities in the family systems of both abusive families and chemically dependent families. These similarities have to do with boundary crossings. In both these systems, the parents' needs are primary. Kids have a sense of role-reversal, where they are not allowed to be kids; parents have very low resources, they don't have a lot of support networks for themselves, they don't have a lot of backup. Kids aren't respected, boundaries aren't respected. The family lives from crisis to crisis, and everybody is emotionally starved. Nobody is getting their needs met. And too often it is the kids who suffer. This system just provides further grounding for abuse of kids in whatever manner—physical, emotional, sexual.

Q. What has the professional community done without this connection and what is it doing now, when this connection is made?

A. I don't know how professionals can *not* make the connection. It is so apparent to me that I can't see why it has been so difficult to get this accepted.

Q. It seems that there has been an acceptance of alcoholism.

A. I think drinking for men, in particular, has been very accepted. You know, releasing the tensions and letting yourself relax, etc. Whereas for women, drinking has had more of a social stigma. I think the problem goes back to abuse. I don't think people believed that abuse happened. I don't think that the women who talked about being incest victims, for instance, were ever believed. People thought it was a myth, and people just didn't want to believe it. At first I think it was just accepted, that men could do what they wanted to do to their women and children. I think abuse is so prevalent because it is the cultural norm for kids to get abused. That is the tragedy.

Q. Alice Miller says that people have always accepted that the parents are right, and if there is anybody who is wrong or "to blame" it's the children. Can you respond to that?

A. Well I think recognition of children's rights is increasing. And I think acceptance of that is the only thing that is going to save us. I think Alice Miller is right when she says that children have been property, that they have been owned by the parents. I think people are just starting to believe children now about the abuse.

The thing that becomes clear in working with people who abuse their kids is that most of them want to love their kids, but many can't. They don't know how. Others try really hard to make good decisions and they strike out—it gets away from them, they are stressed out and they are not able to treat their kids appropriately.

Some of the perpetrators feel five years old inside, they are threatened by adult interactions and they go where they feel safe. And it is a perverse kind of way of getting their intimacy needs met. A lot of perpetrators are consistently drawn to a certain age of kid, and they were that age when their abuse happened. They are that age inside.

What makes abuse so hard to deal with within the family, whether it is emotional, physical or sexual, is that these are people who were supposed to love you and want to give you the best.

Q. Can you elaborate a little about chemical dependency and sexuality? What about the way we learn how sexuality connects with chemical dependency?

A. Part of the problem for me is that I can't separate our sexuality from our social training as women, and men's social training. To simplify as much as I can—the extreme versions of male training and female training are victimizer and victim training. Women are taught to be passive and helpless and hopeless and the nurturers and caregivers, and men are taught to make decisions and go out there and be unemotional, be the financial caretakers—but they are not allowed to have feelings. And women aren't allowed to have power. Society itself sets up the dynamics of abuse. That is not to say men are not abused, because they are, and not to say women aren't victimizers, because they can be. But the social training in itself, I think, sets up abuse. And within that system, chemical abuse or chemical dependency is one way that people try to medicate their feelings about being abusers or being abused. I also think alcohol and drugs lower inhibitions so that people act out their feelings, where they wouldn't if they were sober.

Q. So they are medicating the pain of those roles, the treatment they receive in those roles and the behaviour they dish out, and they are also creating a situation where they can sometimes channel some of the pain to others by acting it out?

A. Exactly. It impacts on every level. Say a girl grows up in an alcoholic family where she is neglected—say her mom and/or her dad is chemically dependent—she grows up being needy, she grows up having unmet dependency needs. "I want to be taken care of, I want to be loved, I really need parenting, I need, need, need." It makes her really vulnerable to abuse outside the home.

   She has spent her life in that role-reversal situation where she was caretaking her parents, where she was the parent and the adults were the kids. So she is used to taking care of adults and she is very needy and she is starved emotionally and she goes outside the home to try to get her needs met. Kids are really versatile and resilient and it puts her at risk for further abuse.

Q. Because she doesn't know the safe and normal ways of getting her needs met? Ways that will not put her in jeopardy?

A. Right. There is so much abuse out in the world. That is the norm. Family is usually the place you go for safety and protection, and if your family life is chaotic and if you are not getting basic human needs met, where do you go? How do these kids get these things?

boundary violation continuum

The following chart describes the range of personal boundary violations which are found in families where alcoholism, drug addiction and/or sexual abuse is present.

Emotional and physical boundary violations consist of family dynamics which lay the groundwork for sexual abuse to take place. Emotional boundary violations are characterized by family dynamics in which enmeshment, boundary ambiguity and identity confusion are prominent features.

"Enmeshment" is a dynamic present in families where little input is allowed. The family is often overprotected from outsiders and underprotected from insiders. Developmental separation is usually discouraged. Because enmeshment drains the family emotionally, a pattern of "disengagement" may follow as individuals separate in an attempt to regain their sense of self. A "crisis" often follows disengagement to bring the family together and return things to "normal."

Physical boundary violations occur when one's body is disrespected or neglected or when one experiences physical intrusions. Covert incest is implied when these underlying dynamics combine with a felt sexual connotation or interpretation. Blatant sexual contract and/or penetration identifies overt incest.

If a child's boundaries are violated, whether emotionally, physically or sexually, there can be some common effects: ambiguity about boundaries, crisis orientation, assuming the victim role, confusion about touch, fear of intimacy, fear of abandonment and the formation of a shame-based identity.

INCEST PRECURSORS: FAMILY DYNAMICS | COVERT | OVERT

EMOTIONAL BOUNDARY VIOLATIONS	PHYSICAL BOUNDARY VIOLATIONS		
blurring of generational lines	adult preoccupied with child's body/ bodily functions	inadvertent touch	french kisses
role reversal		household voyeurism	exhibitionism
parents' needs primary	overly strict household dress code	physical punishment	fondling
unmet dependency needs	excessive tickling	while naked	fellatio
closed system	physical restraint against will to satisfy power needs	sexual hugs	cunnilingus
enmeshment/ disengagement	parent demands physical comfort from child	ridicule of developing bodies	penetration with objects
neglect		putting adult sexual interpretation on child's behaviour	intercourse
overinvestment in child's achievements	touch deprivation		sodomy
intrusions with child's decision-making	physical abuse	lewd reading/ video watching with child	
telling child inappropriate secrets	physical torture	use of objectifying, sexualizing language	
disrespected privacy needs		invasive hygienic practices	
shame-based system			
emotional abuse			
relentless teasing			

what is your story?

E.J.

- I -

Is your story like my story?
My story is the story of more than one child.
It is the story of too many children.
It is the story of pain
    a child's pain
    an adult's pain.
It is a story of lost innocence
       a life stolen
    before the child even knew she existed.
It's a story of betrayal, broken trust.
    A story of secrets, undeserved loyalties,
       lies and threats.
It's a story of abused power,
       control, authority.
It's the story of a child seeking love
                 and security,
      receiving anger and violation
        at the hands of those she loved
        and needed.

It's the story of a child
    who made sense of her chaotic world
      by believing she was bad –
        and deserved to be punished.
    If only she was good
      her mother would return
        from death
      and take away her pain.

- II -

It's the story of a child who tried to tell,
    was called bad, liar, locked in her room
              – alone –
    for telling bad stories.
It's the story of hands and penises
    probing, hurting, penetrating.
It's a story of eyes, fists, belts
    leering, beating, tying
    helpless, powerless
        silent screams
        silent tears.

It's a story of leave-taking
    leaving the self for a better place.
It's the story of a child's terror
              a child's confusion
              a child's survival
              a child's hope and belief
                  in tomorrow.
It's the story of an adult
    who didn't remember
    who hates to remember
    who struggles to remember.

It's a story of physical pain
              emotional pain
      not lived once – but –
        frozen
    to be felt
      again and again.

- III -

It's a story of paradoxes:
    to gain control one must let go of control
    the journey forward is the journey backward
It's a story of friendship, support, caring –
    being called forth
    being empowered.
It's a story about steps
    small steps
        fearful steps –

steps toward freedom.
It's a story of rediscovering and embracing
    the self – lost –
    as a baby, as a toddler, as a child,
    as an adolescent, even lost as an adult.

It's the story of destruction and death
    a story of re-birth and resurrection.
It's the story of child sexual abuse.
It's the story of a journey to freedom
                    and wholeness.

♦

E.J. is a religious sister and a survivor of physical, emotional and sexual abuse. She describes her family as "white, Roman Catholic, middle-class, alchoholic and abusive.

"I spent most of my life wondering what was wrong with me," she says. "When I was thirty I recognized and named the alcoholism in my family and as I untangled that web and broke through that denial I began to realize what happened to me as a teenager was not 'just my fault.' I finally realized that I had been abused.

"Over the past four years many memories have returned involving several different people, many being male relatives and one female. The abuse began when I was a baby and increased after the age of two when my mother died. Since remembering the abuse I have had to clarify my motivations for being in the convent."

finding the answers

Carolyn

"

Alone in my bed I wait and wonder, "Is he coming tonight?" It seems whenever my sisters sleep overnight at their friends' house my father wants to cuddle with me. I don't want him here. I don't want to cuddle with him. My little sisters do. They seem to love him with all their hearts. Why can't I?

I loved my mom so much, but now she's dead and gone to Heaven. I wish she were here. Sure enough, he's coming. I turn to face my body to the wall.

With only his underwear on, he climbs in and puts his arm around me. "Come on," he says, "turn to me. Show me that you love me." I have no choice. Reluctantly I turn. He wants to kiss me. I touch his rough, dry lips with my own. I don't like it. "Put your arms around me." When I do this there is no feeling. I turn again to face the wall, wishing desperately that he would leave and wonder, "Why is he here?"

Suddenly, I feel his heart begin to pound and beat faster and faster. What is happening? Something rises stiff and hard from between his legs. I feel it against me and I feel sick ... He finally leaves.

My father often comes into my bed. Sometimes even after my sisters have gone to sleep. I always keep my back to him and face the wall. His hands try to touch my breasts. I always move away. His hands touch my tickly spot where my stomach does strange things making my insides roll over. It is close to my private parts. His hands also try to touch there. NEVER will I let him. ALWAYS he tries but NEVER will I let him.

Why does he come into my bed?
Why can't I love him like my sisters do?
My father teases me about my breasts. He calls them prunes.
Why does he get so angry when a boy I like comes to visit me?
Why does he kick him out of the house?
When I do go out with boys why does he tease me?

And why do I feel so dirty?

My father and I go away on a trip. I get to go and not my sisters. Will he get a room with two beds or one? I am anxious. I feel funny standing in front of the hotel owner. But he asks for two beds. I feel better. I worry when it's time for bed but he doesn't bother me.

I am not happy anymore. My mom is gone. I am lonely. There is no one to love me. My dad doesn't love me like she did. I play hookie a lot from school. The house is cold but I dare not make a fire. Old Jake Baxter may know I'm home and come over. I stay in my bed to keep warm. I hear someone coming. It's him. He's coming to get water from our well. I hear him call my name from the kitchen doorway. "Carolyn, I know you're in there. I didn't see you get on the bus this morning." He walks in. I crawl under the bed and hide. He stands at the bedroom door and I am afraid. He finally leaves.

Only once does my father show me his private parts. He goes to the bathroom and when he comes out he purposely leaves it hanging out for me to see and walks right in front of me. I am ironing clothes and the ironing board is between us. I feel a little safer. I am all alone. Thank goodness, my sisters walk in the door. He quickly puts it back into his pants and pretends nothing happened.

He always tries to tickle me when I'm doing my homework. I don't like him.

◆

At the age of fifteen I persuaded my father to let me quit school. I was lonely, depressed and suffering from what I thought to be an extreme inferiority complex. I tried to commit suicide once by swallowing a bottle of Aspirins and succeeded only in sleeping a lot. I looked towards my future hoping desperately that someday things would be okay.

I found a job in a nearby town and lived with an older couple. Why did I always feel so awful? I didn't want to live in this world and feel these feelings anymore. There was something wrong with me. I wanted to commit myself to a mental institution. I tried. Standing in a phone booth, I dialed their number. "I would like to commit myself," I stated. What was wrong with me? I didn't know. I couldn't explain. An appointment was made and on that day I paid five dollars for a taxi to take me there. After the tests were taken, the doctor beckoned me to come sit beside him on the couch. I looked at him and saw the wanton look in his eyes. I left as fast as I could down a long, dark hallway with mental patients all around. They didn't want me and I didn't want to be there either.

I find out when I am seventeen years old that he is my stepfather.

I secretly saw a psychiatrist for awhile. If anyone knew they'd think I was crazy, I thought. Dr. Frickner, a middle-aged tall, slender man only sat and waited for me to talk. I had nothing to say. I could not express the feelings inside me. "Do you want to cry?" he asked. I didn't know what I wanted. I left and never went back. No one could help me.

At the age of twenty-one I got married and had two children. I still was not happy. I was fearful, nervous, anxious, insecure and, worst of all, I had no sense of self. Sex with my husband was not the way I thought it should be. I hated my husband for wanting me and disliked it when he touched my body in a certain way.

I could not live like that anymore. Seeing our family doctor to get tranquilizers for my anxiety was my next step. "I feel badly wanting to take pills," I admitted to her. "I believe in God and I am not sure if this is what He would want me to do." She commented about Lot from the Bible, who went through terrible times just as I was, and probably would have taken the pills if they had been available. I left her office somewhat convinced that what I was doing was right and that this was the answer.

The doctor said, "Take them only when you need them." For four years I took them only when I needed them—every day. A few times I tried to stop but always found myself reaching for the phone, feeling uptight and jittery, to order another prescription.

The pills seemed to help. I felt more confident and outgoing. However, I still wasn't happy. I thought it must be my marriage and sought help from a counsellor. In the course of our sessions, he made statements like, "Something traumatic happened in your childhood," and "You are in bondage to something." I was puzzled. Traumatic? Bondage? I longed to know the answers. I left with the resolution that I was going to make my marriage work but the statements still haunted me.

◆

Realizing my addiction and not wanting to be on pills for the rest of my life, I turned for help to the St. Boniface Chemical Dependency Unit. After withdrawal I was left with all the old feelings. They seemed even worse.

My faith was still strong but I finally realized God provides help in trained professionals and that it was time for me to start reaching out. With their help I found the answers. The abuse and my mother's death were the traumatic events that happened in my childhood and the pills were the bondage.

Knowing the answers is half the problem solved. The other is dealing with the effects of the abuse which is the feelings. To do this I have become involved in a sexual abuse survivors self-help support group.

"

♦

Carolyn is thirty-eight years of age. "I have been struggling with the effects of sexual abuse since the age of ten," she says. "At last I have found the light at the end of the long, dark tunnel. I finally feel content, excited about life and my future."

beautiful horses

Bertha

"
*Remembering being there: I'm crying and
I don't know why. I'm afraid. Something is in the room with me. Maybe it's under
the bed. No, no, it is around me. I'll hide my head under the blankets and maybe it
won't see me. Help me, I'm afraid. I better keep my hands in or it will bite them off.*

*I wish my mom was here. I want my mom. I hate being here. Maybe my mother
will come and get me. These people don't want me. No one wants me. I'm so scared.
Help me. Please listen. Don't hit me. I'm sorry. I'm sorry. I'll stop crying. I want
my mommy, not you. I hate you. I can't stop crying. I hate you, I hate you. You're
not my mommy. You don't care. I hate you. I'm not bad. I want my mommy. I'm
afraid to go to sleep. I'm so tired. I don't want to sleep; I want my mommy. There he
is ... OH RUN, BERTHA, RUN ... He's getting closer ... RUN ... I can't run. He's
getting closer. Where's MOMMY? Help me, someone. Help me. I have to run faster. Why can't I run fast? He's getting closer ... Help. Help ... I'm falling. It's dark.
Where am I? Where am I? Oh, oh,*
*I'm here in bed. I'm scared. What's that? The devil's coming again. He's under
my bed. I'll close my eyes. Maybe he'll go away ... Please don't hurt me ... I'm so
scared. I'll think of sheep and horses.*
*White horses, strong beautiful horses. Lots of horses, fast horses. One, two,
three. Look, another horse. He's beautiful and free. The sun is shining. I smell the
flowers and the grass. The birds are singing. I'm free. God, it's beautiful here. I wish
I could stay here. So beautiful. So beautiful. I love it here. All alone with my horses. Free. Happy. Safe.*

When I was a little girl, my mother and father often left me with other
people. Somewhere along the line I was taken away by Children's Aid and
placed in foster homes and orphanages. I was moved over and over again
for the first six years of my life and became uncertain about where I belonged or to whom I belonged.

One day the childcare worker brought me to a home where I was to spend the rest of my childhood. I felt strange and full of wonderment. What was to become of me now?

I remember sitting on a new uncle's knee, laughing and joking about his bald head and asking why there was no hair. I remember a baby with black curly hair and big black eyes. Everyone was making such a fuss over the little baby. I was curious and stepped closer to see what all the fuss was about. I was pushed away. I tried again and was told to go out and play. Feeling felt hurt and rejected, I said, "No, I want to watch too." The response was: "You are a bad girl. Go and play outside. You're such a problem!"

I remember many times "being a problem."

I remember many people visiting and drinking. It was smoky and it burnt my eyes but people talked to me now.

My new parents took me to see my new grandparents. *The old man with the bushy eyebrows and bald head was her new grandfather. He would look at her and his bushy eyebrows would almost cover his little blue eyes. He would talk and laugh with her and sit her on his knees.* I was happy. He started rubbing my legs and putting his fingers in my panties. I could not understand why he did this. *Maybe he liked her. At least he talked to her.*

But his eyebrows and eyes started to scare me now. At night he would come in and play with me. He pulled down my panties and *looked at her and put his fingers in her pee-pee.* Now I was really scared.

One day my new aunt came and asked me if my new grandfather was doing this to me and I said, "Yes." My new aunt said, "Stay away from him. He is not nice." She said that what he was doing was not nice. So I always ran from him. I began to hate him more and more. One day this grandfather died and I was happy.

As a child, I loved the outdoors. I liked to play in the bushes and grass, climb trees and run as fast as I could. I loved to pretend I was a horse; a tall, strong, free horse. I loved to feel the sun on my face, listen to the birds and play in my own world. I became free then. There were no people to hurt me.

My new parents went out at night and left an aunt and uncle to babysit. After a while only the uncle babysat. He would call me *and talk and laugh with her.* Again I was happy, for awhile. *But then he started putting her on his knee and in front of all the other kids put his hand in her pants and played with her pee-pee.* I knew that this was not good, because my new aunt had told me. This uncle was bad just like my new grandfather. I was afraid to move off his knee. I became ashamed and terrified.

One day I went to my new mother and told her what he was doing. She got very angry and made me feel very bad. My new mother would still let that man babysit and he kept on hurting me.

One day another man came to the house, he was a friend of my new mother. *He would talk and laugh and play with the little girl.* One day the man took me down to the basement and said, let's play a game. I was happy. He told me that I had to do what he said or he would not show me his tricks. He laid me on the cold basement floor and told me to lie still and not to make any noise. *He pulled her dress over her face* and took down my panties. I could hear my new mother walking upstairs; the floors creaked with her every step. He said to be quiet. I wanted to scream but was afraid. I could not see anything, I could only hear him say: "Don't move; be quiet." After, he said if I told anyone, he would kill me. I promised not to say anything and never did. I was bad, very bad. If anyone found out they would kill me.

One day I was playing and my new aunt's dad called me. I was afraid but went to see what he wanted. He was sitting on his bed. He called me over and held my arm. I thought he was angry but he smiled. Then he pushed me to my knees in front of him and took out his penis and told me to open my mouth. I fought with him and tried to run, but he got angry and hit me and put me back in front of him. He told me to be quiet or he would tell my new mother I was bad and I would get a licking. Then he put his penis in my mouth and almost choked me. I could not breathe; I was crying and choking but he would not stop. He had me by the hair. All I could do was close my eyes. He went off in my mouth and when I tried to pull away again, he hit me and pulled my hair and told me to swallow. I cried and got sick all over the place; he grabbed me by the arm and told me to clean it up.

I was sick. I was bad and if anyone knew I would get killed. *I hated her.* I thought: "Maybe these things happened because I am bad." My new mother said I was bad, my new father said I was bad. The other kids in this new family said I was bad. At school they said I was bad. Everyone said I was a problem—an ugly black little Indian. I belonged nowhere and no one wanted me. Not even my own parents.

> I wanted to die.
> I hated myself.
> I was no good.
> I was ugly.
> I was black.
> I was an Indian.
> I was bowlegged.
> I was stupid.
> I had small eyes.
>
> Everyone wanted to get rid of me.
> I was afraid of everyone, afraid even to talk.
> Everyone hated me.

I belonged nowhere.
I should be dead. I was no good.

The kids at school teased and laughed at me. I wanted to be friends but they made faces and called me names. I would feel angry and hit them. The nuns would give me the strap and call my new mother and I would get another beating at home. I would try to tell someone but no one listened. They would say I was a problem and bad. I would stamp my feet and try to make them hear, but they thought I was bad and hit me. No one cared.

I hate being alive, I hate myself. I hate them, I thought.
They are all bad, not me. You did it, not me.
I hate you for what you did to me.
    You killed me!
    You killed me!

Today, I know I can go on, that there is peace, happiness and freedom in this world. I know that people can't hurt me, for I've learned control of self. I am waking up to the reality that the world is a beautiful place. It's not the world that is ugly, but some of the people in it. I am alive with the confusion and pain. It's wonderful that today I can feel excited about being alive. It's been a long struggle, but I feel every moment has been worth it. And if things get hard and life seems confusing, I know that, in time, things will clear and my life will shine again.

"

♦

"I am forty years old and of native descent. As a child I never knew any of my biological relatives. I never had an identity. I always wanted to belong. As an adult, I have found pride and power within myself. Today I know I belong. People have always seen me as a strong, hard-working woman—someone who always smiles and is full of life. Inside I am meek, afraid and full of intense feelings. I wear a mask of strength, behind which I am soft and warm. I am learning to connect my strength and my feelings."

being proud of being me

Kathryn

"

         I remember watching television shows
like *The Donna Reed Show* when I was quite a young child. On such shows
the mother was always loving and kind and I remember wishing with all I
was worth that somehow Donna Reed could be my mom. At particular moments of kindness and tenderness, the longing would be so great that it
forced a reservoir of ready, uncried tears past my eyelids, so that my eyes
glistened with a pain and vulnerability that the whole family could witness.

    When I was a little older my mother had a heart attack. Believing that
she was going to die, I approached my kindly next door neighbour and
asked her to be my mother should my own mother die. No one knew the terrible secret I kept hidden. Beneath the surface of my pained expression, I carried joy. When my mother recovered, the kindly neighbour mentioned my
request to my mother.

    Plan A had failed miserably and I promptly launched into Plan B, which
included lying to my mother once again about how deeply I loved her. I
told her that I was worried that if she died, I'd be left all alone with Dad and
"the boys," as my brothers were called, and that this had been too terrible to
contemplate, and so I'd come up with this contingency plan.

    My mother had this strange power over me, so that even if I hadn't
planned to lie, somehow looking into her eyes, the words tumbled out of
my mouth before I could catch them. At these times my stomach would
kind of heave and drop, and a faint nausea would wash over me. It was at
these times that my mother would be very tall, her face far away from mine,
yet bigger than before.

    Sometimes her face would fill up the space ahead of me so that all I
could see was Mummy's face, her eyes seeing through me, boring into my
soul where all of me was kept. She looked this way whenever she asked me
questions. They were strange questions, ones that made me lie or wish I
could come up with a lie. Questions that bored through me, questions that
trapped me into one tiny space where I couldn't breathe. Questions that
stomped around inside of my soul. Sometimes she would order me to pull

down my pants, the questions having led her to decide that I needed to be "spanked." She enjoyed hitting me, always talking in the same insistent voice, telling me that she had to do this, had to, because I was such a bad little girl.

When I didn't go to the bathroom on some unspoken schedule, when I was, as she put it, "constipated," she would hold me down and insert hard grey suppositories up my rectum. My brother helped her with this task, holding me down as I cried out in pain and humiliation. This same brother came into my room at night and shoved other things up my bum and vagina, including his body parts and foreign objects. I was, as the books say, sexually abused as a child. The abuse of me as a child was not only sexual, but physical and, most important, emotional. The interaction between the sexual and emotional abuse was devastating. It left me absolutely certain that all of the abuse that I suffered was my own fault. In my child's mind I believed that I was a "bad" child, irrecoverably bad, and the only hope that I had in this world was to gain the acceptance of my family. If they accepted me, told me I was all right, told me I was their special little girl, I knew in my heart of hearts that then I would finally be "good." Bad girls get what they deserve, and if I ever complained about their treatment of me, they would tell the whole world of my badness. And I knew how bad I was. After all, look at what was happening to me. I was doing "bad things" with my brother. Mummy had to shove things up my bum because I was so bad that I couldn't even go to the bathroom right.

For much of my life right up to my mid-twenties, I looked after my mother. Not only did I lie to her to protect her feelings, I rubbed her back, paid for fancy lunches and dinners out that I could ill afford, and ultimately I did her the huge favour of moving my sexually abusive brother out of the family home and supporting him. At that time I was a full-time student holding down two part-time jobs. I now found myself living with a lunatic.

My poor mother needed a break and I was the one who would see to it that she got one. This same brother was diagnosed as being schizophrenic, when I was about eight years old. I do not fully understand what this diagnosis means, but I do know that my brother treated it as a licence to be even more cruel and abusive than he'd been before the label was affixed to him. He is now in his late forties and is no longer schizophrenic according to the psychiatric community. Yet when I confronted him with having abused me in almost every way imaginable, he blew up, attacked me and used his "schizophrenia" as an excuse. The fact that the abuse started long before this diagnosis was arrived at didn't seem to trouble him at all.

The pattern here is very clear. I was raised to do the bidding of my family members. It did not matter to them then, nor does it matter to them now, that my needs were not being met. For them, being abusive was a way of life. My existence and my pain were not of concern to these people. What mattered was that I existed to be abused at random by four adults.

As an adult survivor of childhood sexual, emotional and physical abuse, I have worked extremely hard to recover myself and to build a life of substance and goodness for me. This process of building a life for oneself is extremely difficult, yet necessary and rewarding. I use the term "recover" because it seems to me that one has to recover the parts of oneself that have been violated, lost or shoved so far away that one forgets that they ever existed. Inevitably some parts are lost forever. There is no way in god's green earth that one can emerge as the person one was born to be, in the face of having endured violent violation. The essential respect that one needs in order to grow is missing. The lessons one learns are the wrong ones. The pain and humiliation take their toll. Fear learned "at your mother's knee" becomes a constant companion. There is no safety. There is no place to call your own. There is no peace, love, joy or family. There is only shame, humiliation, debasement, terror and pain.

This is not the stuff of a healthy mind, body and spirit. This treatment leads potentially wonderful people down the path of self-hatred, self-abuse, substance abuse and often to the loss of life. There is no excuse for systematically abusing anyone, let alone an innocent child. Be that as it may, many girls and boys grow up suffering at the hands of their "protectors and providers." The degree of damage differs as radically as the abused individuals. No one knows why some people end up dead, while others cling tenaciously to life. I do know that I am a "clinger" from way back.

One of the seven therapists that I have seen over a twelve-year period told me that he had no idea how I'd survived my childhood. He said that, by all measures, I should be in some psychiatric institution, not walking the streets being sane and reality-oriented. He used words like "survivor" and "incredibly strong" to describe me. I was never quite sure how I felt about these comments, especially seeing where I'd come from. But they did tell me that I was one of a very special breed. I am a survivor and I am not alone. The streets are filled with survivors. We are taught that in polite company, one doesn't discuss one's unspeakable pain. Over cocktails we smile, discuss the political and economic climate, all the while screaming inside to be heard, to make an essential connection that our shame-based culture will not allow us to make. As a survivor I have made it my business to seek out and establish such connections. It's bad enough that I still carry some shame for having been abused. It's inexcusable that I should ask myself to shoulder such a burden alone. So I do not. As clumsy as I may be in reaching out to the world around me, I continue to reach. I have been abused by my family, by therapists who ought to have known better and by the world at large. Yet I have continued to reach out. The degree of abuse is slowly but steadily being replaced by strong, dignified interactions. Ever so slowly, I am erasing the word "victim" from my forehead and replacing it with "pride."

In my Anglican family of origin, pride is a sin. In my own life, pride is a requirement. In order to heal fully and to grow as best I can, I have to find ways of being proud of myself. Ways of loving me, caring for me, and being proud of being me. I have had to stop looking after my extremely needy and cruel family, and begin to look after myself. This has not been easy. All of my sense of self came from being in servitude, attached to this family, doing their bidding, accepting their abuse and evaluation of me. Who would know or care that I existed if I did not continue to be a part of this "family?" How could I ever hope to be a person, have a life, if I didn't stay around, endlessly working for their approval?

The fear was overwhelming and on the day that I left my parents' house, my brother grabbed onto my ankle and, in order to leave, I dragged him down a hallway and started down my mother's polished oak staircase. I was nineteen or so when this happened and there was no joy, no sense of being a fine grown-up young woman, no pride in moving out and starting an adult life on my own. I was moving because I knew that I would go crazy if I didn't. My father's final words to me as I left my parents' house were: "Only whores leave home without a husband to go to. You are nothing but a cheap whore." Although I hid behind my mask of hollow pride and sent out "you can't hurt me" messages, I was sobbing inside. I loved my parents, something that maybe no one can understand. But I did, and that leave-taking hurt me. There was a huge betrayal in all of this for me. I once again felt betrayed by the knowledge that my family did not wish me well, were not proud of me, did not want me to have a productive life of my own and did not love me. But being the "clinger" that I am, I clung to my decision to leave and to save myself, and quietly left my parent's house.

I am now thirty-six years old, married and planning a family of my own. I feel that I have tended to myself, I have cared for me and I have grown. Finally the idea of caring for another doesn't seem so threatening. Finally there is a light in me, that no one will ever dampen again. The process continues.

I have forged an ending to my past that suits me rather well. I live in a home now. It is not perfect, nor is my life perfect, but it is good. It is a beautiful home that evidences its owners' gentle natures. By and large it is a peaceful home and its occupants live rather peaceful lives. It hasn't always been this way. My partner and I have done a good deal of warring. But at the bottom of all of our pain, there lies an enduring love and respect for one another. We have both worked very hard. My partner has seen me through screaming nights and depressed days. He has worried for me, cared for me like a mother should. He has been petulant and demanding, finding the pain of living with a survivor in crisis to be too much.

I am no longer in crisis. I don't expect that I will be again in the near future. I am worried that my mother's death, when it arrives, will be very hard on me. But I also know the darkest reaches of my soul. I have visited the dark side, I have seen what is there. Most of the time I can handle it.

"

♦

"Since this piece was written my mother has died. Prior to her death, we began a process of reconciliation which, although short, was fruitful. I have no contact with my brothers. At present, I am seeking a creative end to my 'identity crisis.'"

my family and I

Michelle

"
          The basic decision my sisters and I had
when we were children was to choose how we were to be abused. It was ine-
vitable that if we refused the sexual abuse, we would be knocked around or
totally cut off from friends or anyone outside. We were able to cope with
this because we had each other.

I was a middle child. I tried to protect my sisters, especially my younger
sister. I was thrown down the stairs once for trying to protect her. If I refused my father's sexual advances, he would just move on to another sister.

Between us four older sisters, we had comaraderie, a support system, the
feeling that we had allies. We also had a sense of love for one another. We
used to get together in one room and talk and let our anger out. We talked
about how we felt and about possible solutions.

Reporting to the authorities was the most obvious solution. We tried discussing it with my mother and there was no help there. She would hold up
articles from the newspaper about a father charged with sexual and physical abuse and the family being broken up and she would say, "Is this what
you want?" We tried discussing it with relatives. There was no help there
either. Everybody just confirmed that this was to be kept a secret. Therefore
we had to depend on ourselves. Every once in a while we had to help each
other when we'd go through things like suicidal feelings or wanting to run
away.

I found the biggest pressure I had to face was knowing I had the power
to go to the police or an authority figure and confess what I was experiencing. My mother wanted to keep the family together and we considered her
our saviour. My sisters and I didn't want to break up the family either.
What we wanted was help to learn how to be a healthy family. But there
was no such help available.

So the idea of reporting to the authorities was far too much pressure for
me to take on. I was in a no-win situation. I turned the abuse inward,
usually in a destructive manner. I would run away from home or think of
suicide. I would have long term

depressions. The most positive thing was being able to talk to my sisters, to have somebody to verbalize it with and feel safe.

◆

As a child I was taught to always be responsible, always think of the other person first. I always put other people first, which made me feel worthless.

◆

When I confronted my dad about the sexual abuse he expressed a lot of denial. He said he never intended to hurt me, and that he didn't hurt me. I would respond by telling him that he did hurt me and not just in physical ways. Often he will ask, "How was I supposed to love you?" It's very simple in my mind: love me as a parent does a child.

I think abusers want to have a release from their guilt. They want to hear that they didn't hurt their victims. It is not my responsibility to tell him that. I wasn't asked as a child how I felt. No one helped me deal with my feelings, except my sisters. His key excuse was that it was the only way he knew how to love us.

◆

My father is still a denying alcoholic. I had to use alcohol in my life to survive the pain.

◆

My relationship with my parents has changed over the years. When I left home, I resented my parents strongly. After I got married, there was a total cut-off. For two years I never spoke with or saw my parents because I felt such resentment and anger. I just couldn't get rid of it. In the meantime, I'd had my first child and it made me focus on all I had missed as a child. I also understood my parents from a parental perspective. I know it's difficult at times to be a parent and I tried to envision myself in the same situation. Would I protect my children at all costs?

◆

Now that I see my parents aging, I want them to acknowledge that they made mistakes. For the last few years, I've been trying to be open and honest, and not to be so worried about hurting their feelings with the truth. I always tell my parents I love them very much but I did not love how they raised me. It was wrong.

I want to have contact with my parents but I don't want to pretend anymore. My parents are still in a state of wanting to pretend, to forget, saying they want to live their old age in peace. But it's important for my healing to have them acknowledge that they were wrong, that they caused a lot of pain and anguish, and that they are responsible. Not just my father but my mother as well. She was the person who was supposed to keep me safe and protect me. I was her baby and she left me to handle the abuse in whatever way I could.

To this day we have a lot of love for our parents—respect is another matter. There has been no admission of guilt. They always say: "That was the best we could do." I have told my mom, "I have more hate for you than Dad. He was ill!

◆

In school I was often a zombie. These days I think they notice things more and try to deal with them.

◆

I think everyone has to have a sense of belonging and roots. And I find it a waste of energy to build up a lifetime of resentment and avoidance when I'll never have another set of parents. I can try to turn this situation around into something positive. We can unite our family by being honest with one another. I've never been able to share any of these deep feelings with my parents over the years, and now I can. I want them to understand the mistakes they've made. It's very healing for me to be able to go back and talk. Although my parents ask why I am hurting them like this, I tell them it's not meant to hurt.

But I've had a lot of hurt for many years and I'd like to deal with this and be able to share with them how I felt. Maybe they can share with me why they made the decisions they made, so I can understand that it wasn't just that they didn't care about me. Maybe I can have my family love even yet. Now, while there is still time.

"

♦

Michelle is thiry-five, a divorced and remarried mother of four children. Two years after she wrote this piece she says, "I am at peace with myself. I had a major breakdown two years ago and had to face the abuse in my past. I always had depressions but the last one was the worst.

"What started my depression was that my father approached my eldest son (sexually). The approach was subtle but that's how it starts. It was like reliving the nightmare. My ex-husband and I were breaking up. The school was aware of what had happened and I was afraid it was all going to come out in public. I was so trained in denial that public disclosure was one of my major concerns.

"I severed the relationship between my son and father. I rarely see my parents. I was hospitalized for four months—I emptied out in hospital and when I got out I had to start all over again. It was so hard. I was spiritually empty and suicidal. I phoned crisis lines. When the man who is now my husband first tried to get to know me I ran away from him. I always ran from the nice guys.

"It was always hard to get love from my parents but I get love from my husband, who is a very special man. He listens to me talk, he holds me, and he cries with me. He is wonderful to me.

"Now I am a very strong and aware parent. My kids have always been my guiding light. I pay close attention to hug them and talk to them.

"I learned about how to love with my children. I am learning from my new husband what it is like to be loved."

no simple problem

Amanda

"
At the age of fourteen I was molested by my grade eight teacher. What I thought to be simple attention turned into a nightmare. I knew nothing about sexual gestures. I couldn't understand why a married man in his field would want anything to do with a kid. I remember him repeating over and over how he cared for me, like he was trying to hypnotize me as part of his fantasy. I felt so used, betrayed and worthless.

It was toward the end of the school year on a school outing that his gestures became touches. I felt trapped with nowhere to go. Then it came out into the open. Everyone knew what was going on, what had happened on the field trip and what had happened throughout the school year. The child welfare agency was called in to investigate.

Now that I look back at it, I realize how poorly the situation was handled. I remember walking into the principal's offices and being pointed to a chair in a roomful of people. My heart pounded, my stomach turned and my eyes began to water. I was so afraid. I wondered what was going to happen to me. I couldn't look at anyone. I kept my eyes on the principal.

Then the questions came—one after another. They never gave me a chance to answer, it was as if they were trying to confuse me. Feelings overpowered me but I answered as best I could.

That was it. I was sent back up to the classroom, like a piece of old rag no one wanted to know.

Counselling was set up for the summer months. I was to go and talk to a counsellor about how it started, when I didn't even know myself. The first time I went she asked me to tell her what happened. The next time I went the teacher was in an office nearby and the counsellor told me his story was different than mine. I blew up at her and left. That was all the counselling there was.

In counselling I was asked one question to which I now wish I could change my answer. They asked me how I would feel if the teacher lost his job and his family including "his little girl." Already feeling guilt and shame, I said I didn't want to be responsible for a little girl's unhappiness. I knew the unhappiness I felt growing up without having a real father. I couldn't do that to her. So he was let off. They played on my guilt and shame to keep me quiet. They cared more about the abuser than they cared for me, the abused.

My parents didn't even know I saw a counsellor. I thought they had been informed of the whole situation but I was too embarrassed to bring it up. So when I went to counselling I had just said I was going for a bike ride.

When I went to high school the teacher who had done all that to me was there. When I ran into him in the halls I would panic and go another route. Once downtown he tried to approach me. I went the other way.

He never apologized to me about what happened. The last time I talked to him, just before it all blew up, he said he didn't mean it to happen and "what could he do?" He told me he cared for me more than his wife. I didn't want to hear these things. I was only fourteen. He was eventually transferred to another province but I feel sorry for the students he is now teaching.

Two years after the counselling ended, a school counsellor asked my nephew how I was doing. He asked in front of the whole class. I believe his lack of confidentiality is totally unprofessional. I feel that it was wrong for him to talk so openly about something that caused me so much pain. I feel sorry for other students who confide in him with similar problems.

I now find myself angry at all those teachers for their unprofessional counselling, for how they took advantage of me and how they didn't inform my parents. I believe the reason my parents were never informed was because they wouldn't have been intimidated, like I was. The school authorities wouldn't have been able to make them feel guilty or ashamed, like they made me feel. There would have been a requirement to do a lot more.

A problem I now have is that I work in a public place and see other teachers from my former junior high school almost every day. They stare at me and give me dirty looks. They make me feel like a freak.

When I got married there was a lot of pressure because things weren't working out very well. I started having nightmares, reliving the same story. My bond with my husband was not the same as it had been before we got married. I had difficulty being intimate with my husband, which depressed me. Enjoying intimacy made me feel ashamed, guilty and afraid that I was going to be used again.

I went to a medical doctor and explained these problems. She asked, "Have you been molested?" I broke down and said, "Could this (the relationship I'd had with my teacher) be causing the problems?" She said it could be, and she referred me to a counsellor.

The counsellor helped me deal with my feelings, my emotions, how I felt about it—not just the incident with the teacher but a family incident as well. I have been attending a group for women who have been sexually abused. It has helped me to open up, to realize I am not the only one, that it is not my fault. It was only through counselling that I told my parents.

Even though I've finished group therapy I don't think things will ever be fully resolved for me. What was thought to be a simple problem, easily solved, has had a huge effect on my life.

"

♦

Amanda is twenty-two years old, works and is planning a family with her husband. "We are doing fine now. I deal with 'it' (the abuse)—that's how I think of it. I still have to deal with the effects of abuse a lot. But my husband and I are getting along. Our marriage is stable and the bond we had before marriage is re-established. My husband was very supportive through my counselling. He was there for me all the time. I thought he would think I had asked for it (the abuse).

"We are planning to have a family and I think I will discuss with my kids the do's and don'ts of their bodies. But I am still scared. You hear of so much sexual abuse happening. I don't trust people very much. If I have kids I will worry all the time about them. It is my husband who really wants children. I'm not so sure."

grandpa why?

Chickadee

Grandpa why?
You're not supposed to do that
Grandpas aren't supposed to do that
I remember you
Tall
Kindly
Mustached
Grizzled
You played pat-a-cake games with me
You taught me how to play chess
Now I can't play without remembering
Grandpa why?

this time I tell

Chickadee

Grandpa why?
Why have you come back
To haunt me again
I thought I had left you
And the broken wall
far behind
But now
Out of the blackness
Of night past
You come again
I desperately try
To rebuild the wall
But caring hands
prevent me
I must turn and face you
Live it through again
Feel it again
Confusion–
Fear–
Pain–
But this time I tell
And the magic spell
Is broken
Your power gone
I shake you off
And walk away.

barely a ripple

Chickadee

Skipping stones
Watch them sink
The ripples spread
and then they're gone

I watch myself
in little pieces
tossed about
at others' whims
Hurting wildly
no self direction
barely a ripple
then I'm gone

♦

"I was sexually abused by my grandfather from the time I was three through to my teens. My daughter and I were also emotionally and sexually abused by my husband. I ended up depressed and suicidal. The last eighteen months have been a journey towards healing.

"The key factors in my struggle have been people. A key person for me has been my counsellor, who has gently and patiently helped me to explore and express my feelings, to sort out my options, and to reclaim my life. My church family also stood by me. At times, when I was overwhelmed by my problems, my faith weakened. My church friends were always there, supporting and encouraging me. Without these wonderful people in my life I would not have survived."

— K.G.

methods for surviving

interview with Sue Evans

Part Two

Q. Sue, can you talk a bit about the cycle of shame and blame that people can get into. What is it and who gets into it?

A. Well shame is really an interesting phenomenon. I think that growing up in a family where people are emotionally starving and nobody is getting their needs met—not the parents, the kids, nobody—then a lot of times the kids, when needy, are blamed for it. Their job is to take care of people, their job is to not be needy. Kids need a lot. They are very time-consuming and energy-consuming. And when you are battling an addiction, you don't have that kind of energy. So you push the kid away.

If a child's identity is shame-based, the child feels that she is wrong—that something is wrong with her inherently, as a person, rather than with her behaviour or because mom's drunk today, so don't ask for anything.

In simplified terms, what happens when you have a shame-based identity is that more energy is put into ascribing blame than is put into accountabilty. In other words, if you can blame someone else, they are bad instead of you, and you get a sense of relief. Even if it's just five seconds of "put the blame on somebody else," because if you can't blame somebody it comes back to yourself. You think, "Well, then it must be my fault." And so a shame/blame system is impossible to get out of. But people try. They desperately try to pin the blame on anybody but themselves.

To change, to operate within an accountability system, you have to get yourself out of the habit of viewing things from the perspective of "who's bad, who's great, who's wrong," and allow each person to say their part. Accountability is saying, "Well, here's my part, how I contributed." And the other person says, "Well, here's my part and that's how I contributed. Where do we go from here?"

Shame/blame is saying, "Well, you did this" and "No, you did that," and it is continuous and there is no end.

Q. Can you explain the spiral quality of shame/blame?

A. Sure. Shame experience feels like an attack from within. Say that you were always shamed for being needy as a kid, or being angry or being sad or whatever it is that was unacceptable in the family. Then whenever you feel that as an adult, it is an automatic trigger for shame. You come close to feeling needy and all of a sudden you have a shame attack. In a shame attack, the tapes of how bad you are start running. "I'm so fat, I'm so dumb, I'm so _____" Fill in the blank, everybody's got their own. And it feels totally real. A shame attack is totally believable. We look around desperately to explain why we feel so defective: "Well, I crossed the street at the wrong place—that's why I feel so bad." And it really is just a shame attack. The damage is in how we are mean to ourselves in our heads. It makes us off-centre, it makes us ready for another shame experience. People are so cruel to themselves in their own minds.

   And so the spiral part is just cycling down: being mean to yourself, feeling absolutely abusive to yourself and feeling that it is true, that you deserve everything bad you ever got in your whole life. And the only way to protect yourself from it is through rage, or trying to deny the whole thing, or blaming somebody else. Different people have different tricks that they find are more or less successful.

   Rage is a common link with shame. In a rage attack, you feel more powerful, you feel strong, you feel you can blame somebody else because they are really screwing up, but it is really a defense against feeling so awful, feeling so defective. And it just feeds on itself, it's contagious ... one person being shameful can trigger another person's shame and it's really a massive, massive undertaking to get out from under it.

   So I think it's crucial to realize that if you grew up in an alcoholic family your chances are close to 100% that you have a shame-based identity. And certainly if you have been in an abusive family, you have definitely been in a shame-based family.

Q. So you would suggest that people who recognize that this pattern fits for them should try to be aware of it and know that the accountability model is more productive and safer?

A. Right. But it is a totally alien concept. When you are in a shame cycle, it feels impossible to have any sense of accountability because you are just so busy trying not to own everything.

Q. Does shame/blame originate in an abusive family so that a child will never be able to think that the parents aren't parenting? So that it will appear that parents aren't accountable for their parenting? And is that why children don't learn realistic accountability either?

A. Exactly.

Q. How do you shift to a healthier relationship model?

A. In the model that I work with, the first step is acknowledging the shame: "This is shame, it feels awful." Label it, notice that you are shameful. Because a lot of people have shame experiences and don't even know it. They just walk around full of rage, or they walk around being mean to themselves or whatever. So label it, acknowledge it, stop the inner abuse—a hundred million times a day it's going to take. It's like a conditioning, you hear how bad you are over and over and over. You are going to have to counter that, catch yourself and stop the abuse, then neutralize it, say something nice to yourself, give yourself affirmations and then go on from there and try and start over.

Q. Sue, can you talk about your own evolution in dealing with chemically dependent women who are adult survivors of childhood sexual abuse?

A. In the early days I was very clear about the victim process and how unfair it was that these women had experienced what they experienced. I saw them as being in need of care, nurturance and support. I spent years and years listening to the horror that women have survived ... it is just heart-breaking. Years and years of listening to the atrocities that women have endured had the effect of making me see abusers as monsters. I probably provided therapy for ten years using the "pure victim" approach. You know, "Look at what's happened to you. Feel the feelings of what's been done to you."

Q. Why is it important to "feel the feelings?"

A. I think that people use coping skills to get through the abuse, to live through it. Women have endured things that would kill, and somehow survived it. There are tricks that people have used and one is to deny the feelings. Another is to pretend everything is okay. Another is to create multiple personalities, where a whole other personality comes into being and takes over because you don't know how to live through the abuse, you are too little. So going back and claiming the experience, feeling the feelings of what's happened, is part of the recovery process. You can't just "wall off" a whole part of yourself, you can't repress selective parts of yourself—if you are repressing pain you are repressing joy, you are repressing sexuality, you are repressing your ability to be excited and happy. If you are repressing, it is across the board. So if you go back and claim the pain, you also get to go back and claim the joy, the childlike wonder, the excitement. It is a major part of the recovery process.

Q. You were saying that for many years in your work you dealt with the victim.

A. With the "pure victim" approach. And when I did my masters program I did an internship in the program of human sexuality at the University of Minnesota and they asked me to work with an offenders group— child molesters and incest perpetrators. It horrified me. I was scared to death. I had spent years hearing about these monsters and now they wanted me to go into a group? Besides, I had my own history of recovering from abuse. So I thought long and hard about it and I decided to do it. And I think it is the best thing I have ever done in terms of my work with victims.

What I learned in doing the group was that these people are just plain people who are in trouble and who have really horrible and damaging ways of acting out the pain, but it is their attempt to get their needs met. There is a very small percentage of these people who are the psychopathic and like to inflict pain. But by and large these people are trying to deal with their pain, trying to reach some connection with another human being. It's perverted, but the abuse is an attempt at intimacy.

And that was so important—to see these people as victims themselves. It changed my entire focus. So when I went back to my clients and worked with their victim issues I could say, "What the perpetrators do is monstrous, but they are just people." It knocked them down to human level. It helped me to see how the "pure victim" approach was keeping people in the victim mentality. It helped me to offer a sense of empowerment. It allowed me to guide women into the next phase of their recovery.

Q. What would that be?

A. It allowed me to hold victims accountable for their lives now. If I saw the perpetrators as monsters and the women I was working with as victims only—there was a ceiling on their development. They would always need to be afraid of these monsters. They would always need to be stuck in their cycle of rage and blame and they never had to push themselves to be accountable now for their lives. There was a helplessness in the victim mentality, and I wasn't pushing them past it because I didn't know that there was some place beyond it.

Q. So, when you were looking at the victim only, the picture was incomplete?

A. I think by seeing how perpetrators are victims, I saw how victims have learned the victim-victimizer system. And by holding them accountable for their behaviour, a whole realm of accountability was opened up for victims. Yes, they had been victimized but that didn't mean it was okay to victimize other people or, as is most often the case, victimize themselves.

Q. For instance you?

A. For instance me. Which was regularly happening, in their anger and their rage. And I would think, "Oh well, that's okay. I understand you have been hurt."

Then I realized, "Well no, you don't get to hurt me no matter how much you've been hurt." And by understanding that perpetrators were victims, I set some limits. I understood that victims have learned the exact same system as perpetrators. They have learned how to perpetrate. It may be more subtle. It may be not as clearly acted-out. And I think, in fact, that stems from the difference in our male and female socialization. Men act out their pain, women tend to internalize it. Or come at it indirectly. So this understanding was a missing piece. It moved me into a more systemic approach because every person in the scene has a part to play. And that is not to say that victims are in any way at fault for the abuse that occurred to them. I want to make that really clear. But it does say that the system is like a mobile with everybody balanced perfectly and you can't be a victim without perpetrators and you can't be a perpetrator without victims. And you take one out and the whole system ...

Q. One of the things about being a victim is that you have never been asked to be accountable in any normal way. You have always been asked to take the entire rap, the entire blame. That's not what you mean by accountable?

A. Being accountable now doesn't make you responsible for abuse. The abuser is absolutely responsible for his or her part. It doesn't mean you are to blame for it. It does mean that you need to look at your behaviour now, to make sure you know what your part was and to make sure it doesn't happen again.

   Accountability is very different from blame. I think the only way out of a shame/blame system and the only way to heal from it is to say, "This is what I did. These are the signs and this is what I've got to look at the next time."

Q. When you compare the behaviours and feelings and values that fit in the shame/blame system to those in the accountable system—you are basically living in a different world.

A. Right. From my own personal experience, I was married at a young age, to a man who was abusive to me physically, and I went into therapy saying, "Look what he has done to me ... " It took months for the therapist to turn that around to where I could say, "Look what I have allowed to happen to me and I'm not going to do that. I have some power here and now to make a decision about how I want to live my life. Yes I love him—well so what!" And it's a major turnaround. It doesn't mean that it's my fault that I got hit. It means I must ask myself, "How do I want to live now?"

possession

Ruby Tuesday

The talons
of cruelty
beckon
gleaming
     in the light
outstretched
scalpel sharp
capturing
prey of heart
and then
shredding
     to atoms
the delicacy
of mind.

such a little girl

A.M.

Such a little girl
to be imprisoned
in fear and guilt
threats and blame.
The silence
slowly building bars
around her.
As the outer girl grows
the little girl is forgotten,
her screams are shut out
misunderstood and frightening.
She wants release,
yet, the silence
she has learnt
stills real communion
with the grown woman
who doesn't recognize
the pain
or where it is coming from.

♦

"I am in my thirties. Over the last two-and-a-half years I have been actively healing wounds from the sexual abuse and incest I suffered from several perpetrators, as a child, teen and adult. I had blacked out most of the childhood abuse.

"It has been a painful journey. I feel myself growing spiritually and emotionally and becoming the woman I was created to be. I know that this journey is worthwhile and lifegiving."

pain, strength and hope

C. P.

"

I sit here looking at this empty page and wonder how to begin to put my story on paper.

Most of my childhood is a blackout. Around ten or eleven years of age, I was sexually abused by someone I trusted in our neighbourhood. For two years all the neighbourhood kids, including myself, hung out at this old man's house every Saturday and sometimes after school. We called him Old Man Tate. He was in his early sixties, and he lived alone in this house off the back lane. He was a junk collector.

One rainy Saturday morning I went to his house. He asked me to come inside and offered me coffee. I was the only one there that morning, but it didn't bother me because I trusted him. We talked and he showed me the odds and ends in his house. Several hours went by in this way and then he approached me, talking softly and saying he wanted to play "doctor."

I can only remember flashes of what happened next. I remember him removing his pants and telling me it was okay to do this. He told me to lay down on the bed and he removed my pants. He stroked me around my belly area. He kept saying, "Trust me, I won't hurt you." Then he got on top of me and pressed his penis against my vaginal area.

When I look back at what happened I remember feeling very frightened and lost. I recall looking at the side wall and sinking into it. I felt the pressure of his penis and then he got off of me and wiped off the bed. My next memory is of being locked up in his basement. He had a trap door on the floor. I don't remember how I got out.

The thing I remember is running home. It was very dark outside. I went into the house. My mother approached me and told me I was late for supper. She was mad at me for being so late. I started to cry and she asked me to tell her what was wrong. I told her but I don't remember what I said.

I remember being interrogated by two detectives. They asked me questions and questions about what had happened. I felt they didn't believe me because they said, "Are you sure?" Even the look on my parents' faces said they were in doubt. During this whole time no one gave me any support or comfort. I remember being very upset and feeling alone. I found the cops were very cold and insensitive to my being upset. Now, when I look back, I feel angry with the cops about the way they treated me, as well as angry with my parents.

I recall the police saying that I had to go to the hospital to be examined by doctors. I vaguely remember going to the hospital. I felt so much coldness being in that dull room with bright lights shining from the ceiling. The doctor came in and said he had to check out my private parts. I didn't understand completely but I recall crying a lot. The doctor shone the lamp onto my vaginal area and I felt something being inserted inside of me. It hurt and, by this point, I was screaming for them to stop it. I remember the nurses holding me down on this small table—with my feet stuck in a sort of buckle strap at the end of the table.

All I could see through my wet eyeballs were strange people looking down on me. I felt like a piece of meat being butchered for display. I remember the nurse injecting something into my arm to calm me down. I don't recall my parents being in the room when this took place. I felt there wasn't any support or sensitivity for how I was feeling. I felt so alone going through this crisis in my life. No one asked me how I was doing or even gave me a hug to say, "It's okay."

The neighbour kids heard about what had happened and I found them backing off from me. A lot of kids said I was a trouble-maker and a liar. I felt hurt and abandoned by my friends. Shortly after the abuse happened, Old Man Tate confessed that he did it. There were reports of other cases of children in the neighbourhood who had been sexually abused by this man. Apparently they were being investigated. Tate was found to be insane and put into a mental institution where he died a couple of years later. Some of the kids blamed me for his death.

I did feel badly about him going to the mental institution. Sometimes it's like a circle spinning around in my head because for a period of time when I was young, I trusted this man, and he betrayed that trust. Sometimes I can't believe that it happened because I like him and had fun over at his house on Saturday mornings. Then reality hits me in that I was betrayed, hurt and trapped emotionally and physically by a person I knew and cared for.

My father started sexually abusing me when I was around fourteen years old. I remember the first night clearly. I came home to tell my parents I was in trouble with the law. Two months before I had been out of town with two friends and their mother at a cottage and we got into trouble.

That night my mother was playing bingo like she always does six nights a week. My dad was sitting on the couch. I knew I had to tell the truth soon because the guilt was eating me alive. I remember walking into the house and feeling afraid to tell. I decided to tell my father before I told my mother.

(I was very afraid of my mother because she physically abused me. Once she took six belts together and hit me wherever she could. Also, I was afraid of her emotional abuse. She would say I wasn't good enough and I was a stupid person. I was afraid I'd be locked up in my room for a week or weeks on end.)

My father was a passive type of man who never took responsibility in raising us kids. He seldom disciplined us. Ninety-nine times out of a hundred, he would sit back while my mother would be totally aggressive with us. Still, I thought I would tell my father and hope that he could calm my mother.

So I told my father I needed to talk to him. He looked at me as if he knew what I had done wrong. He looked up at me and said we should go upstairs and talk. He seemed so calm. I was walking behind him, going up the stairs and, at the top, he said we should go into my parents' bedroom. He sat up on the bed with his back leaning against the wall and his legs lying on top of the bed. He told me to sit on the edge of the bed. My back was half-turned towards the wall and I was partly turned towards him. I then burst into tears and told him what I had done wrong. I said I was really sorry and felt badly. I told him that it had happened two months ago. He told me that the RCMP had phoned him, told him what happened and when the court date was set for. I started to cry again and to express my remorse.

Suddenly he reached over with his right arm around my right side and grabbed my right breast. I immediately stood up in shock and looked at the wall. Then he got up and said he was sorry and not to tell mother. He said he would take care of telling my mother about me and the law. He knew I was scared of my mother. Also, I now realize, he was feeling guilty about the sexual assault and out of guilt he decided to take care of it with my mother. As well, his help would keep me quiet about the sexual abuse.

For the next few months, my father left me alone. Then one day he started to talk to me in a soft voice and asked me to listen to his problems. He confided in me, about his sexual problems with my mother. He said my mother was frigid and had cut him off sex about five years previously. (At this point in my life I didn't have a clue about sex. My mother strongly put it down as being a very bad and dirty thing. Sex always has been a taboo subject in our family.)

I remember my father saying it was a human thing to do and that he needed help. My father confided in me that he had gone to a hooker to help him release his balls, but he told me that he was not happy because he couldn't get his penis hard. Then he told me about seeing a girlfriend concerning his sexual problems and she couldn't get his penis hard either. He said if he couldn't get a release soon that his balls would enlarge so big that they would explode and he would die and that I was the only one that could help him. He said I was the only one left to help him. I believed my father because I didn't know anything about sex.

Then my father showed me what to do with his penis. He took my hand, placed it on his penis and showed me how to give him a hand job. A couple of times while I was doing this, he touched my breast. I remember his sperm shooting out. When he made me clean it up I felt so sick to my stomach. Also, I realized that every time he wanted me to give him a hand job, his left eyebrow would flicker up and down. It would make me want to crawl into the wall and hide. Oh, I hated this abuse from my father! I remember the feeling of him coming on to me once or twice a week for about two years.

Today, I believe my father sexually abused me because I was vulnerable during and after the sexual abuse by Old Man Tate.

Then one day my father told me he was running away from home and not to tell my mother. He told me the day on which he was going but he didn't tell me where or to what city. One Monday morning he left me a note, that said he was leaving on that particular day, and five dollars under my pillow. I went to school feeling sick to my stomach because I was the only one who knew what he was up to. You see, my mother had tried to overdose on drugs in the past, and I thought she would again try to kill herself.

When I came home from school, my mother was upset to find the runaway note from my father. I remember my brother being there and trying to calm her down. That evening my mother decided she wanted to end her life. She took an overdose of prescription drugs—she had plenty around the house. (My mother is a drug addict and gets her pills from doctors.)

I remember sitting in the ambulance watching them pump my mother's chest in order to help her breathe again. The siren came on when we went through intersections. I was scared that my mother would die because of me.

Because my father strongly advised me not to tell anyone, I then found myself feeling afraid of both parents. To this day I know that my father shouldn't have dumped that responsibility onto me when he left home. Now I recall saying to my father, "What is mother going to do, try to kill herself?" It seemed it didn't matter to him. He just wanted to run away from home and dumped it all on me.

Sometime before my father began to sexually assault me, I started to sniff glue and nail polish remover a lot. It got to the point where I needed to use it at school and after school. Around this time I started to steal my mother's pills from her bedroom. I couldn't cope with learning in school and being in class with other kids. I didn't have a clue how to be around other kids. Doing drugs and drinking made me feel part of the crowd and I got some attention from my booze buddies. The drugs and alcohol made me feel secure and gave me confidence.

From my childhood on, I felt that everyone knew about the sexual abuse. I felt ashamed, dirty, unwanted and alone. My school marks started to get worse when I was eight or nine years old. Then they progressed to very bad and I was just transferred from one grade to the next. I was failed a few times. The kids used to call me "stupid" and "dumb". So did my whole family.

As time went on and I felt more alone, abandoned and scared, I did more drugs. Self-destruction started to become a way of life for me through taking drugs, alcohol, cutting myself and shutting people out of my life. My life became more unmanageable through my teens to mid-twenties. I started to fix needles in my arms and hands, with drugs like speed and cocaine. My alcohol problem also became worse, life became very foggy. I tried to kill myself in different ways: like cutting my wrists and arms, and taking overdoses of street drugs and prescription drugs.

I felt I had no life at all except for pain and rejection. I felt I wasn't worth anything, and felt unloved and not cared for. When I was young I was told I wasn't worth anything on a mental, physical and sexual level, so that's how I saw myself.

There were days that I didn't know if I was coming or going. I became a cold, tough human being because I felt I didn't belong anyway. When I was under the influence of drugs and alcohol I did some crazy things to get attention. I started to break the law, especially when I was high on dope.

I found myself starting this pattern of going in and out of prison. At this time, I felt that I had nowhere to go and this was home. Also, jail reassured me that I was a bad person.

I was heavily into drugs and alcohol for about twelve years. The chemical dependency stopped my mental and emotional growth. I had a few close calls with death in my mid-twenties. I almost died a few times and this has turned out to have helped my spiritual growth, because my life flashed in front of me. I started to learn that I wanted to get help. It was like a sign that I was meant to live. Anyway, it scared me enough to start changes in my life concerning my drug problems.

A couple of years later, when I was off drugs and alcohol, I started to have feelings. I wasn't sure what they were, but I knew I needed to learn how to cope with these feelings. (Up to this time, I drank my feelings away.) I started to see a therapist. At times I felt I was going crazy. My feelings were so great I was almost frightened to death. I hurt so bad I would crawl along my apartment floor trying to find a safe place to lie. It got scary when I couldn't find that safe place. I knew I couldn't turn to chemicals but—I tell you—it was a struggle to stay sober and clean from drugs. I also got support to stay sober by going to a group for alcoholics, and that helped. I had to take one day at a time, and even one second at a time, just so that I would not grab that first drink or drug. I feel grateful today that I started to see a therapist back then. She eventually helped me to look inside, feel feelings and identify them. She told me it was okay to cry. I was afraid to start crying because I was afraid I wouldn't be able to stop myself from falling apart. Slowly I allowed myself to cry.

Flashbacks about the sexual abuse started to occur. My feelings were so great I wanted to die. I realized that I did not want to die physically, I only wanted the feelings of pain to die. I got involved in two sexual abuse groups and one mixed group where we dealt with our hurt, anger, betrayal, and our inability to trust. I found that writing it down on paper helped, as well as talking about my pain and thoughts with someone I trust. I found that important when I released some of my pain from deep in my guts. What would I do with that empty space? I just cried. I said healing statements to myself like: I, C., am lovable. I, C., trust myself. I am okay. I love myself.

I started taking the attitude that I was responsible for how I was feeling and therefore I would do what I had to do to survive. This emotional work takes time but I don't want to feel like a victim anymore. The more I release my feelings, the more I regain my power as a woman in this world. It takes time to heal inside and I realized the connection between my drug and alcohol abuse and the sexual abuse.

When I was younger, the chemicals stopped my feelings, especially when I was around other people—I couldn't cope with one-on-one relationships. I feared being hurt, and mistrusted people because of the sexual and emotional abuse. I didn't trust the medical profession, the police department or my family. I felt I could do things on my own through drinking my life away. Back then, I stopped growing.

Now I have some awareness of how I feel and what I can do to take care of myself. To me, this means staying sober (one day at a time) and reaching out to safe places and people. I did some therapy for about a year and then stopped. Now I'm back doing some more work because I still have flashbacks. I know that if I don't deal with these feelings I will end up drinking booze and doing drugs to push down the pain. I know enough about myself to realize that if I grab that first drink or drug I may not come back alive. I will be emotionally dead or I will commit suicide. If I do come back alive I will be like a vegetable. Alcohol and drugs are powerful stuff—they kill us, and they kill the emotional pain in us.

Sometimes I feel the hurt and pain so deeply that I don't know if I can make it alone. I have recently set up a support system so I don't have to be alone with this pain. Sometimes I get hope from other women sharing their stories with me because I feel I'm not alone in my pain and struggle to stay alive. Sometimes when I feel the effect of the abuse and how it has hurt me, I feel rage and then I try to get to my bed and beat it up. I would rather hit my pillow than cut up my hands and arms. I scream at my pillow, or whatever, as a release.

I now see that chemical dependency and emotional dependency go hand in hand. Since my last slip, I have been sober for almost three years. I feel proud of this. I believe staying sober takes courage and guts. We all deserve to pat ourselves on the back for being honest. We can all work together to share love and support. Writing this has given me hope to carry on in my life. I'm still learning everyday coping skills and sometimes I find this to be challenging. For myself, to feel feelings and to be sober is the greatest high in my life today.

I took a trip across Canada a few years ago so I could see relatives that I hadn't seen for almost sixteen years. I wanted to find out about some missing pieces in my family tree. During my trip, a lot of things got validated for me. I realized I wasn't crazy and that it was true about the abuse happening. Sometimes I feel rage when I hear people from my own family saying to me, "Yes, we thought something was wrong back then. Oh yes, we saw you being treated like a black sheep." I have wondered *why* they didn't step in and take me out of my home? I just want to say I was a victim of people's ignorance. And also a victim of the way society dealt with child abuse in those days, and still does today.

We can work as a team to help children who have been abused, by educating teachers, principals and the police, and teaching parents about child abuse on all levels. For parents, this would include learning how to identify signals and how to ask children questions, as well as teaching our children about verbal abuse and bad touches. We should teach them to tell someone if they have been approached, to phone a children's help line or someone they trust. And we should teach them to say "no" to strangers. I also strongly stress that children should be aware that the abusers can be their fathers, uncles, siblings and relatives. We need to educate young people about child abuse, before they have children.

As well, I must stress that if you have been abused as a child, get help before you hurt someone else. We need to deal with our own issues before we have children of our own. We need halfway houses for children and young adults who were sexually abused, as well as for those who have been involved in drug and alcohol abuse. People are dying from the pain they feel inside and they need a place to work on their pain.

Child abuse has to be stopped. We can start by talking to each other and being aware of what is happening next door. If you see or suspect child abuse, phone. You can save a life. Yes, we have to make child abuse our business. I wish that someone in my past had made it their business. The solution is to put our ignorance aside and open our eyes and minds and our hearts to others.

"

♦

C.P. is thirty-six, single, and at the point of "sharing my seed of hope with others. I have trained as a crisis volunteer and am also starting work soon at a detox centre." She has been working in a non-traditional field but now prefers to work with people rather than in the trades. "I have a wonderful dog and work that I think is valuable."

drinking and drugging:
don't talk, don't feel, don't trust

Zoe

"

My natural father died when I was four years of age. (I do not remember him as he spent long periods away from home gambling). When I was five my mother remarried, to a man who was eight years younger than her. He paid a lot of attention to me. Although I had two siblings, he called me his favourite. Later I was to ask, "His favourite what?" This man, whom I now was calling "Daddy," fondled and kissed me in a way that repulsed me when I was old enough to understand it.

Our lives centred around keeping this man "happy." I came to loathe the parties my parents held. Actually, it was what happened after everyone went home that I dreaded. My stepfather beat and verbally abused my mother after each and every party.

I remember meals that were eaten in silence—you could virtually "cut the air with a knife." My mother would very often have tears running down her face during the course of the meal. My father's face carried a brooding, unyielding and angry look that I came to fear.

We lived this way for a very long time. The drinking, abuse, sexual fondlings and disharmony caused depression in my mother and migraine headaches in my brother. My sister (the eldest) became my mother's confidante and I came to be the "invisible" child with many signs of insecurity. These included rocking incessantly to prompt sleep, nail-biting, withdrawal, fantasizing (talking to and nurturing my dolls), and constant scratching which required medical attention and resulted in my introduction to prescription sedatives.

My stepfather constantly criticized me. I developed feelings of inadequacy and insecurity. I did not feel that I was capable of doing anything right. I learned that my feelings were insignificant and so was I.

And so it came to pass that I would marry very young, feeling that these troubles would be left far behind me. However, my husband and I had grave difficulties from the start. We both were immature emotionally and

70

the responsibilities of marriage overwhelmed us. We had intimacy problems that we could not resolve. When my children were four and two, I left him to venture out on my own.

My old problems were traded for new ones, and I even added a few more. I was very lonely and could not stand to be alone with my children. I pub-hopped with girlfriends who were either divorced or separated. I abused alcohol at least once a week (I could only afford to go out once a week) and met many men. I seemed to meet men who were unavailable to me for one reason or another (they were married, or could not commit to a relationship for other reasons). For ten years, I lived in limbo, fighting off depressions by curling up in the fetal position and sleeping my life away when I wasn't trying to cope with two children, a job, being both a bread-winner and a social butterfly.

Then I met a man who was to become my second husband. Our relationship was totally destructive in that this man abused me constantly. But I was sure that if I loved him enough he would stop or get help for his hostility at the world. He convinced me to marry him and even though my instincts told me that it could be disastrous, I went ahead with it. I rationalized that he had given up drinking and that he was "into change." I blamed the battering solely on his drinking.

My husband had a long history of incarcerations. He had been married twice before. He had battered his previous wives and had a history of alcoholism. He drank excessively and lived off me like a parasite for three years. He also physically abused my son while I sat crying in the corner, feeling helpless and too hopeless to stop the cycle of abuse. I was outraged that I had paralleled my life with my mother's. I felt I had been cloned.

During those years of knowing him, I felt certain that I could "save" him. It did seem that I had a habit of seeking out relationships in which I felt I had to "work" at finding acceptance and approval ... just as I had with my stepfather.

With many years of battering, verbal abuse, and alcohol abuse, I finally managed to see that my efforts to get this man "help" were going unheeded. I recognized that my life was unmanageable and my relationship with my children was deteriorating. My daughter showed signs of withdrawal, depression and, in general, I think she did not trust me to do what was right by them. My husband had also fondled her ... the cycle was starting all over again.

"

◆

Zoe joined Al-Anon and with the support of this organization and a psychiatrist she terminated her marriage. Her relationship with her daughter got back on track and, she says, "For the first time in my life, I am enjoying my own company."

Zoe took a number of counselling courses and does volunteer counselling. "I took a Life Skills course which involved learning to trust one's own feelings, trust of others, intimacy and expressing feeling. I learned a valuable lesson here about accepting other people's feelings, and in being in control of myself only. I went on to Distress Line Training and all the previous learning was reinforced here. I became involved with a Women's Support 'Share and Care' group. I co-facilitated and then facilitated the group myself. While doing this I took a counselling course at the university and did very well. Now I do volunteer work as a lay counsellor with people who have been victimized. I'm better at understanding my father's addiction to alcohol and my mother's co-dependency, and even my own co-dependency. I have a wonderful rapport with my kids now. We are friends, we can hug and say 'I love you' without feeling squeamish."

Zoe is presently working as a secretary for a psychiatrist. She is forty-six.

splitting to survive

Me

"

                   I sat alone with God in the agony and darkness of my shattered spirit. During this reflection and grieving, my unknown parts were rejoined by a miracle. What follows is my journey to inner union, written in a state of which I have no conscious memory.

Innately I know I am loved and wanted before my very conception.
My arrival one snowy November day is greeted with great celebration.
Outside I am healthy in all ways, and female in physique.
Inside I carry a spirit bursting with impatience to live and to love.
The celebration belies the reality of where my spirit will journey.

I will learn to mentally and emotionally deny the torture I lived through at the hands of those who celebrated me.
I will learn to deny physical pain and smile in frozen terror.
I will be anything anyone wants, at a moment's notice.
I will live from instinct and information.
To do this I learn to kill my spirit before they do.

the mother's dream

As I grow I become sick, with colic, pneumonia, growing pains in my knees.
I am to be the perfect girl-child to complete the mother's dream.
Perfection does not get sick and I feel betrayed by my body.
I feel the mother's rejection, disappointment and frustration,
Her anger: "What's wrong with her?"
I accept responsibility.
I kill a "bad part" of my spirit.
I still grow, and now talk.
Perfection looks pretty, obeys, sits quietly and never cries.
It does not ask questions or touch things.

It does not play in the mud or laugh too loudly.
I feel the mother's impatience; inadequacy, not knowing the Answers.
I feel her shame at my behaviour.
Her panic at her failure of motherhood.
I accept responsibility.
I kill another part of my spirit.
The child who is creative, curious and spontaneous is now gone.
It saves me from feeling crushed by rejection.

daddy's princess

I continue to grow.
Daddy calls me "Princess."
He brings me little hotel soaps from his many trips.
We bang nails and take care of our goldfish together.
He teaches me to fish—just me and my dad.
I love my daddy, he is my only source of affection and attention.
What's left of my spirit feels good with him.
Until he invents "Our Special Game."
He sneaks in my room at night, smiling.
"Hi, Princess. Make Daddy feel good," he says.
So I do. I am little and innocent. I love my daddy.
I do not know it is wrong till the mother tells me.
"You're lying. Your father would never do that. You're crazy and don't
ever say that again."
The sheer terror is too much for me.
"Mommy says I'm crazy and Daddy's not really doing that. Okay."

I call kilroy

Daddy used to be gentle.
Now his probing fingers hurt.
It hurts when he puts his arm on my throat to keep me silent.
My head hurts from banging on the wall as my little body rocks under-
neath his.
The physical pain and total confusion are too much.
I call for Kilroy. My friend who will never leave my side. My friend who
will share my inner torture for thirty years.
From His grace He will bless me with no memory of Daddy's game.
My salvation is to be able to split my tiny spirit in two.
The good one for the world, and the bad one to be buried.

I live from my head, never feeling again.

I learn to look away from Daddy and put myself in the wall, or fly around and watch from above.
Sometimes I keep Kilroy company up on my toy shelf.
Till Daddy goes away.

the perfect little girl and the whore

As I leave my body, what's left becomes someone else.
A self I will not know for thirty years.
All that was felt, heard or seen will be stored behind a steel door in my mind, where my bad parts live.
I somehow create two new people.
The perfect little girl and the whore.
They work from inside and I will not be consciously aware of them for a long time.
They cause me to act, but are total strangers.

The little girl talked too much once and the mother tied her to a chair.
She didn't cry—she played dead and waited patiently to be untied.
Now she is a robot—perfection.

The whore is there for Daddy's game.
She became too perfect and very smart.
She could sense things well.
Mommy's unhappy—Daddy's lonely.
"It's okay. I'll make him happy."
She was the limp, lifeless body, Daddy touched and licked and raped.
She became my unconscious depository of slime, torture, memories and silent screams.
She held it all in loyal silence from the little girl.

I am ten, we move and the game ends.
I continue to grow in body only, going through life numb, and silent in smiling obedience.
Oblivious to my inner agony.
I am fourteen and he has a heart attack.
I watch in terror as he gets drunk, home only hours from the hospital.
Inside me, someone screams, "Oh no, not again."
I am confused. "Not what, again?"
He drinks. She drinks.
We all fight.
I tell the truth again, "Stop drinking!"
He beats me up.

She says, "If you could just shut up, he wouldn't get upset and have chest pains. If you were a better daughter he wouldn't have a heart attack and die."

I accept responsibility.

alcohol weakens me and the whore escapes

So that I don't feel the self-hate of believing I have the power to kill someone,
Unconsciously I summon Kilroy, the whore, and the little girl.
It worked then, it should now.
But it doesn't, I have no energy.
So I drink alcohol to kill the panic of failure.
But the alcohol weakens me and gives the whore an escape.
Drunk, she uses my hands and body to feel good the only way she knew how.
She gains control over her hell by abusing men's bodies.
She is flashy, confident, cunning and brave.
She is fearless and powerful and loves to flirt.
Men are toys to be played with, a never ending stream of challenges to be conquered.
Her moment of triumph is the smile of sexual satisfaction on a man's face as she laughs and thinks, "Another one down."
Drunkenness is her world.
In sobriety she hides in my bad space inside.
The hung-over little girl wakes up and tries desperately to deny the stories her friends tell her.
"That's not me. I'm perfect. I'm not a whore. I would never do that."

My brain and body live in separate worlds.
The little girl feels self-disgust but has no memory of the acts.

I am nineteen and Daddy dies.
I get drunk to celebrate my freedom from the king's reign.
He is dead and so is the whore.

I marry and gain respect. The little girl has all she's dreamed of.
We drink and party for many years.
The little girl still waking up wondering, "Who did those disgusting things last night?"

The husband is very confused.
Little girl sober, whore drunk.
But the brain is very good at manipulating his confusion with her excuses.

I take pills for the headaches

I have a baby and stop drinking.
He is loved, wanted and celebrated, as I was.
I take pills for the headaches that cover my unfelt inadequacy and failure as a mother.
I am addicted—I hit bottom and throw myself into recovery.
Driven by the shame of my stupidity, I am oblivious to what I will find inside myself.
My child would not be silenced as I was.
He spoke loud and clear. "This is crap and I deserve better."
By a miracle, I listened and agreed.

as I grow so do the fits of rage

I grow and change and make decisions.
I leave my marriage and accept responsibility.
As I grow, so do the fits of rage,
Along with a horrible haunting feeling that says, "There's much more."
Little by little the flashbacks come.
Then pictures, then words, then terror, then feelings.
My brain fights like hell denying it.
"My family is nice. If this is true, why don't I remember it."
The little girl cannot bear it for a long time.

Slowly the brain looked and listened.
I felt horribly confused, tricked by my own mind.
I felt crazy and cheated, angry and hurt.
Worst of all, I felt totally betrayed by myself, my parents and God.
Who could be trusted now?
I felt nauseous with shame.

one day I felt the little girl

Counsellors said, "This is the most courageous work you will ever do. You need to get to know the little girl and love her. She was helpless and innocent. She had no choice."
My anger and fear said, "Bullshit. I hate her. She's a god-damned little brat."
I was incapable of even imagining a journey of knowing and loving her.
Despite my hatred, one day I felt the little girl.
In the presence of someone very gentle, she appeared.
She is small and I can't see her clearly.
She is distrustful of me so she stays distant and can't speak with me.

Innately I know she holds a part of my spirit in her hands and it is safe with her.
But that's all I know.

I work and struggle hard to get to her but I can't. I want her, I need her but she won't come.
I dream of a steel door that leads to a long dark swirling tunnel with a black pit at the end.
She is at the end.
Out of frustration I choose to open the door and go through the tunnel to her.

as I open the door, there stands the whore to greet me

In all her power she laughs.
"Remember me! Well, it's either both of us or nothing."
I want to run back to the safety of my denial.
I want to escape her evil.
"You're dead!" I scream. She laughs.
"You kill people. You're slime. You do disgusting things to men.
You're not part of me. I'm nice."

The shame and self-hate fill my being.
I want to die.
I spin, I cry, I go numb.
I try to force her away, but it's too late.
I confront her. We look at each other as strangers.

Despite my hatred, I feel the whore around me as I did the little girl.
Somehow, inside, she holds the other part of my spirit and it is safe with her.

split is safe, whole is an unknown

By a miracle, I am present to all the parts of me I killed.
My brain, my whore and my child, brought together by Kilroy, who never left us.
I tell my counsellor.
I think it is the end. My brain is feeling "in control" of all these psychological puzzle pieces.
They say now I must choose to be split or whole.
Split is safe, familiar.
Whole is unknown.
I accept responsibility and choose whole.

I am given two women to walk through the tunnel with.
One for the little girl, one for the whore, and Kilroy for me.
They are safe and caring and can be trusted with all my parts.
They teach me these parts are not psychological but spiritual.
They are good spirits who just made some bad choices.
The women tell me, "Yes, these parts are strangers to your brain.
They had to hide or you would have been killed."

I learn kilroy is god

I learn he took a part of my spirit and kept it alive, that not all of me was killed.
I learn that from that small, alive part can come the love and courage to welcome the little girl and whore back into my heart.
Most important, I learn that I alone can choose to let them out of the closet of horrors they live in.

I accept responsibility and begin.
I freeze in panic.
It feels real. I'm crazy again. I can't stand the confusion and the fear.
It hurts too much.
My self-hate grows into suicidal thoughts.
Yet that small alive part keeps saying, "You're safe now. You lived through the worst before. Hang on, just a little more."

Time passes and I am numb again.
My memory does not remember things in the now.
My body is exhausted.
My friends and family are confused.
I scream and cry. "No more God. I can't do this. I'm not strong enough."

But I keep going, I can't make it go away anymore.
I am driven now by that small part that screams louder, "I want to live, damn it. I want to live."

I enter an agonizing, dark aloneness inside.
I feel emotionally shredded by a past invisible pitch-fork.
My body feels like I'm carrying a ball of barbed wire inside.
I experience mental blankness.
I have no sense of time passing.
Then one day I feel something so deep inside I question its existence.
I write till my arm aches.
I learn somehow, someway, sometime we have been re-united—my parts and I.

I talk to them, hear them and work very hard at accepting them.
Upon embracing them I will feel the pain that was never felt, see what my eyes could never see, and know what my mind could never know.
They tell me they love me and need me.
They say they never left me.
They were always there within me, just out of my mental awareness.
They say they hid to protect me, so as not to do something wrong that I would have suffered for.
They say they have lots to give me if I allow them.
They want life too.

the little girl is innocent, the whore is strong

The little girl is innocent, compassionate and loving.
The whore is strong, capable, brave and very determined.
Sometimes I cry from gratitude and sometimes I sit in awe of these parts of me.
There's been both agony and ecstacy in this first step of inner healing and union.
I know now they have been loyal and truly carried me through horrors I could not live with at the time.
I feel safe and grateful in the knowledge they held my spirit in their hearts till I could learn to live in it with love and honesty.
This is our beginning.

Now, by choice and faith, I am learning to show my parts in the presence of two women and God and others as well.
I am learning to hate what was done to me, and not hate me.
I am learning very slowly to love me as I am and as I was.
My parts and I are safe now to feel, to remember, to cry, to scream—whatever is needed is accepted with respect on our way to wholeness.

the gifts of our union are many

The freedom of voice to break the terrified silence and say what I couldn't before;
The freedom to feel, instead of numbness;
The gift of a heart to listen with—the unfelt hatred surrounding my heart is breaking away to allow love to enter;
The freedom of choice—I never have to be forced to do anything again.

II

♦

"Alcoholism and incest were separate issues for me. I am an alcoholic and an incest survivor. I am an alcoholic because I have the disease of alcoholism, as my father did. I believe alcoholism is hereditary. When I reflect back, I realize that I took my first and last drinks, and all those in-between, like an alcoholic— with an innate vengeance.

"In my teenage years I instinctively related to boys sexually and acted out what had occurred between my father and me. It was an innate pattern and I was skilled far beyond my years. I lived out the same pattern with my husband. I was a passive, obedient sex machine on 'ready alert' at all times.

"I believe I would have become an alcoholic even if I hadn't been an incest victim. My alcoholism developed without anyone's actions affecting it. I progressed through the stages, quit drinking and now maintain a daily recovery program. Incest as a child governed certain behaviour patterns which have continued all my life.

"When I began my recovery program years ago I quit drinking and using, left my husband, remembered my incest and dealt with it. I now work full time. When I entered therapy I never thought I'd get to where I am now.

"I started to 'journal' at the beginning of my therapy. It was through writing that the real me, inside, would find the courage to appear. It was in the silence and safety of writing that I learned what I think, how I feel, and who I am. In time, it was where I would have contact with my split selves and get to know them. And it was there, in the privacy of paper, that I got in touch with the Dad I had known in childhood. Writing became a place for me to vent my feelings and organize and check my perceptions. It became the only safe place I had known since childhood. Writing became a major support and friend.

"I am still in awe of the journey I have taken.

"I have learned not to look at the future too much. Other than knowing I want to get a degree and a house for my son and me, I live one day at a time. I have to. In my thirty-eight years I have wasted too much time and energy running from the past. I choose life moment by moment now.

"Speaking as an alcoholic, I believe God wants us to be happy, joyous and free. As an incest survivor, I believe He wants us to walk in self-respect and dignity, in our journey of happiness, joy and freedom."

wishes

Andrea

"

     After I was assaulted by my brother and became enmeshed in an incestuous relationship with him, I made attempts to tell my mother. She disbelieved me. The little girl I was back then was never comforted. Instead she was blamed. This hurt me in an excruciating way. My father's anger at who I became drove the hurt deeper. That wounded and betrayed little girl still lives inside me. What follows is a collection of "wishes" that have been presented to me over the years by the little girl inside me.

my mother

My mother stands back, unbelieving, proud of her eldest, a son. She doesn't believe me, doesn't allow herself to accept that he's not perfect. That he is touching, feeling, inviting her insecure middle child to take her clothes off, assuring her that nothing will happen. It's just a game the university students play and it makes her feel so grown up. Mature! Beautiful! Wanted! OUT OF CONTROL! My God, what's happening? Something is terribly wrong! It feels good, but it's not supposed to. Knowing that, the guilt begins to grow.

    The thought of my mother creates an uneasy feeling deep inside. There is confusion—I love her but I don't think she loves me. I want her to understand what is happening to me and how I feel. But she thinks I am making up stories. I HATE HER!

    Do you remember Mommy, when I told you that something happened to me? You told me, "Don't say things like that!" and "Oh, don't be so silly!" and "That's not true!" Do you remember Mommy? Now that I'm grown up, Mommy, sometimes I wonder—do you believe anything I say? Do you love me?

    Sometimes, Mommy, I wish you believed me.

my father

My father was very authoritarian, very autocratic. He used to say things like, "No man wants used goods" and "Men only want to marry virgins, not somebody who has been around!" (I wonder what happens to little girls who are used against their will? Does anybody want them?) My father's word was law. And I believed every word he said. After all, he was The Father.

♦

After she was assaulted, the little girl became cautious and frightened. She lost her sense of belonging and became angry and rebellious. That annoyed her father and he got angrier! He thought that she was intentionally being a thorn in his side.

He began yelling at her and accusing her of many things—things that he had earlier taught her were wrong, evil, bad. He said she was lazy, took drugs and "ran around", whatever that was supposed to mean! He became very cold towards her.

Sometimes, Daddy, the little girl wishes for warmth.

my older sister

When asked to describe my older sister, these words immediately come to mind: admirable, respectable, sophisticated, happy, in control. The feelings that come to mind are: jealousy, envy, love, a sense that I can never be as good as her, as beautiful, or as worldly. Sometimes I feel she puts me down. For instance, when I try to explain the incest to her she invariably replies, "Oh for God's sake, that happened a long time ago. Stop dwelling on it and get on with your life!" (Is that what you would do, dear Sister? Would you not feel the pain, the embarassment, the humiliation, the lack of self-worth? Don't you realize that it's comments such as those that lead people to commit suicide?) I feel so incompetent when she says that! I don't think she means to hurt me. I think she has a difficult time accepting that something like incest could happen in our home. I think she hides behind the belief that "dirty" things only occur to those in the lower classes of society. Dear Sister, don't you understand that your denial only contributes to the dysfunction of the family?

Sometimes, Sister, I wish you would accept me and what happened to me.

the little girl

The little girl looks at the woman and all that she has gone through. She remembers how, not so very long ago, the woman was inside of her, protecting her, helping her to block out the pain. Now their roles are reversed. Now the little girl is the protector. She helps the woman understand that she is strong and able to handle most situations. She helps the woman deal with her emotions. Often when the woman cries, the little girl cries with her.

She thinks about the men the woman has chosen for partners. Without fail they have been men that she can control. That control is usually destructive, and the little girl helps the woman to realize that. She gently guides the woman to understand that drinking brings only temporary relief from the pain. She teaches her to use her skills, her talents, her creativity, as a means of expressing and relieving the agony she has lived through.

I wish for you that you will find and listen to your little girl.

II

♦

Andrea is a thirty-five-year-old survivor of incest. For most of her adult life she has worked in the helping professions. She is an aspiring writer and single "by choice," she says.

"I find I need to spend a lot of time alone. I am most at peace when alone on a beach on an overcast day. Some days are bad and some days are good."

pain

E.J.

When will it end?
Will it ever end?

Pain
   so deep
I cry out
      but no one
         can hear.
Pain
 rising and
    bubbling
 pushing its way up.

Pain
 it can't be kept down
  it will be heard.

Pain
 healing tears
 will one day flow.

Pain
 part of my
   life
I must accept.

Pain
 it will end
    I cling
      to hope.

anger

E.J.

that burns within
eating away
seething and boiling
ready to erupt
to wipe out everything
in its path.

Anger
that wants to lash out
hurt, destroy.
I cannot
I must not
let anger control.
I must not destroy or hurt.
I must bottle it up.
Anger must be hidden.

through a child's eyes

E.J.

Through a child's eyes, I saw the fear,
Through a child's eyes, I felt her tears.

Of a secret she held deep inside,
Something so terrible, she just,
wanted to hide.

I knew she wanted to trust me,
As she tried to speak,
But she was bound to the secret,
She was trying so hard to keep,
For so long she had blamed herself,
And carried the guilt, that belonged,
to someone else.

Too young to realize, that it wasn't,
her fault.

That shame belonged to a trusted adult,
who had abused her, before she could know,
She had a right to say NO …
But now I know.

I cried tonight

E.J.

I cried tonight
   not momentous
      for many.
For me
   it was.

A child—a small child
   was hurt real bad.
She lost her tears.
They fell on deaf ears.
They were beaten away.
They were ridiculed,
 until they came no more.

Now I've found them
   I hope
      I never lose them.

— K.G.

healing

interview with Sue Evans

Part Three

Q. Can you zero in some more on women healing, accountability, and also how women have learned the victim-victimizer system, and what the process is for looking at that, and how it is healing?

A. When I helped women get in touch with their victim selves and the un-fairness of that situation, I think some women knew that they had vic-timized other people, even if it was only by hurting themselves. When you make it "them versus us," the monsters versus the victims, I think they can't heal. They can't face the feelings of what happened to them, they can't feel the feelings, because deep down they believed they were part monster themselves.

Most often women who have been victimized tend to act out their victimized behaviour on themselves. This increases depression. Women will sometimes physically hurt themselves—even slash themselves with knives—to relieve the pressure of the shame/blame and carry it to some kind of conclusion. Teaching them to take care of themselves, not to abuse themselves, is a first step in recovery.

When you put it into a systemic approach where everyone has been victimized in certain ways, everyone perpetrates in certain ways—be-cause the rage that you feel is certainly strong enough to make you want to hurt others; when you can acknowledge that you've done harm to others, I think then you can understand in a deeper, more healing way, how you've been harmed. People don't have to split monster ver-sus victim within themselves, because they know that they have got enough rage to perpetrate. They know that they, on some level, have hurt other people—out of their own pain. And when they can accept that, they can also accept that the victimizer—their victimizer—has also been a victim. And it moves things to forgiveness, forgiveness of them-selves, forgiveness of the system—not acceptance, not, "Oh well it's all right that I have been victimized." I don't want in any way to imply that. But it leads to a personal resolution, forgiveness of themselves.

Q. I can't help bringing up Alice Miller again. She says that when victims of childhood abuse spend time understanding their abusers, they are immediately unable to retain their feelings about what it was like to be totally terrified and invaded by the abuser—be it a parent, a more distant relative, friend of the family, stranger—whatever.

A. It's a balancing act. In the first stages of healing it is very important to be totally in touch with the inner child, the child that was abused. People need to feel their pain, rage, fear—all the range of feelings they have from the abusive experience. But eventually it helps the victim to get the inner child out of the system by understanding the context of abuse. This by no means lets the abuser off the hook for heinous behaviour.

Q. What are your thoughts on forgiveness of perpetrators?

A. I think women in general want to forgive too fast. It's part of our training, it's part of our being other-oriented, seeing the other person's point of view. It's also a defense against feeling the pain of abuse. You know, "It didn't really hurt me that bad—poor guy, poor guy." I think there are lots of reasons why women want to forgive too soon. I always challenge that, because there is important work, important feeling that needs to happen first—with the sense of betrayal, the anger, the sense of total outrage that "they did this to me." And so if people are trying to forgive and hide stuff and avoid doing that work, I challenge it.

I think that people can get stuck in blame, too, though. People can try not to take responsibility for their lives today because they think, "I've been hurt, I never deserved a job that I feel good about, I never deserved a family, I don't ever get to be in love, etc." There is identity in being a victim. Some people get stuck saying, "Well you hurt me so I get to ... " And that is destructive to them. So my goal is to see that the victim comes to some understanding of the system. If they can get to real forgiveness when they have done all the other work, then that's good for them. For their own comfort and the easing of their pain.

Q. Can you talk a bit about how it comes about that it is time for a survivor of childhood sexual abuse to forgive?

A. Forgiveness should only happen after the victim goes through the phases of feeling their own feelings about being a victim, goes through the anger and rage, goes through being accountable and then goes through how they have victimized themselves and/or others in their own lives. If, perhaps, they go through confronting the abusers, bringing the family in, confronting the people in the family who did nothing about the abuse, talking about it, getting true to themselves about what happened and the effects—I think in some cases that allows the forgiveness to come. Certainly it makes a difference if the abuser(s) say(s), "Yeah, I did it. I'm sorry. I know I was wrong. Will you forgive me?" It's much easier for the woman to say yes or no or whatever. It takes a big person to forgive when the abuser looks you in the eye and says, "No I didn't do it. You're crazy. I don't know what you're talking about. You've always been the whiner in the family."

It takes a big person to say, "I know you did it. Too bad you can't admit it. I forgive you anyway. You are a sick person."

Often I don't see that part of it. Often a person will be years out of therapy before they work through to that point. And often they never do. It is for them to decide.

Q. Can you talk about the impact if, in error, a therapist, or any other person who is influential in the victim's life, pushes for forgiveness?

A. I think that it circumvents the work that needs to happen. And it is usually an attempt by the therapist to medicate the victim's feelings. For example, the therapist may be intolerant of the deep emotional work that needs to happen. Or it strikes the therapist's own abuse issues, and she/he doesn't want to feel it. Or it strikes his/her own abuser issues, for that matter. That is common too. But it is very detrimental to women because they end up feeling that there is something wrong with them— how come they are still mad, and how come they can't do it right, how come they still want to drink? How come they can't accept this "happy ever after" thing, now that they've forgiven? And they feel, "Now what? I still want to shoot the abuser."

So it is very destructive. I think it is a denial of the reality. Again, it is the person who has suffered the abuse who knows if they want to, or can, forgive.

Q. Can you talk a little about people having feelings that they didn't allow themselves to have when they were being abused and what happens developmentally for them?

A. I believe that when a person experiences abuse they kind of stop developing. There is a part of them that keeps on growing and dealing and going on—but you can be an adult and have a little kid inside you that is living in the abuse. So, if somebody comes up to you and puts their arm around you because they want to be close to you, you're fearful: "Oh my God, I'm going to get hurt again! I don't want to be sexual." The kid exists in that moment.

And you have to go back and rescue that kid, so to speak, by going back and feeling the feelings, saying to that child inside you, "Yeah. I know. And I'm going to be there for you, I'm not going to let anybody hurt you again and I'm not going to abandon you." Because when we went on and left the kid back there, we left the kid with the feelings. The feelings were too big and we said, "Unh-uh, not me." We left the kid in the cellar and going back, feeling the feelings, is like saying, "Okay, come on, you're two years old or you're are four years old. I'm going to treat you like a kid who is four years old. I'm going to take care of you, I'll feed you, and here, have a doll." You do all the nurturing kind of things that the kid needed then, when nobody was there. We need to do that as healers. And I think the kid grows up and jumps to the next stage. And then you say, "Hey, I'm eight years old! What does an eight year old need? And what does a fifteen year old need?" And so on.

So you grow those parts up, developmentally. I may be too concrete in my description of that. But exercises like writing letters to the kid, and writing letters from the kid inside, writing letters from the kid to the perpetrator—they allow that part of you to have a voice, they allowing the feelings to come out so you're not so split apart inside. If we push the feelings away, we're cutting off whole parts of our selves. (And it's understandable why we do that.) So we're increasing communication between the adult self and the cut-off, blocked-away parts. These techniques are not like throwing open the door and having the flood of experience and living it. But they start the process. I think they're just claiming back parts, claiming back the good, bad and the ugly.

journey of renewal

A.M.

A cleansing
of the recesses of the mind
of all the hurt and guilt
accumulated through the years,
a slow process,
a sifting process,
a painful process.
Oh, the courage it takes to embark
on a journey of renewal.
Oh, the nurturing of self
that is needed,
as each new wound is opened
to let the festering sore be cleansed.
The mind resists sharing
the secrets it has harboured
preferring to masquerade.
A cleansing
A purifying.

megan's story

Megan

"
My story begins at the age of four. My
father loves me very much and he protects me from my mother who is often
very angry with me. She hits me a lot and calls me a problem and a trouble-
maker. I think she might really hurt me if my dad was not there.

I love my dad a lot. We work in the garden together and he talks to me
about ways to help things grow in the garden. I spend a great deal of time
outdoors with my dad. He teaches me to recognize different birds, their
nests and eggs. He loves nature and so do I.

My dad likes to hold me. Sometimes, when he is on shift work and sleeping during the day, I sneak into his bedroom. He cuddles me and touches
my body all over. I like the way it feels and I feel wanted, but I am afraid my
mom will catch me in there and yell at me or hit me for disturbing my dad.

As I get older, my dad touches me more and more. His touches become
probing and I start to feel a little bit afraid and uncomfortable about what he
is doing. I am uncertain and I don't think I like it.

Sometimes when my dad and I are gardening, he will start to touch me. I
go into the coal shed with him. His hands move quickly over my body. His
caressing and touching is very thorough. He takes his penis out. I don't like
this part. I am afraid but I can't run away. He puts his penis in my mouth
and I choke but he moves it around in my mouth. He pulls it out and turns
his back to me. After a minute he says, "Come on, Megan, we've got work
to do in the garden," and I go with him like nothing at all happened.

Lots of times when my father does these things with me, it is after ar-
guing with Mom, usually about something I did. While they argue my
father tries to defend me or protect me. Sometimes, my dad looks really sad
after he does these things to me. I pat him on the cheek and say, "It's okay,
Daddy. Don't be sad. I love you." I always feel tired afterwards. I feel afraid
and I want to hide. But still I would rather be with my dad than with my mom.

When I am about six or seven years old, my father's best friend visits us.
I enjoy sitting on his lap and being cuddled. We walk down the road to the

woods beyond our fields. As he holds my hand, I show him the wild-flowers. We walk into the woods. It feels cooler there. It might be late spring. I don't remember when my dad comes there or even if he walks with us, but he is there.

The next thing I remember is being on the ground. They are both touching me everywhere—rubbing my body. My underwear is off and my dad is touching me between my legs. He rubs his penis on my face and puts it in my mouth. I choke and gag. I am so frightened. At first I am worried that Mom will be angry if I get my dress dirty. Then, I am very scared. I want it to stop! They threaten me with a knife—a fishing knife, I think.

"Don't tell anyone, Megan. Don't tell!" I want it to stop and I promise I won't tell.

I feel so bad. I want my mom to help me so I decide to tell her it was just my dad's friend. Maybe she will believe me. But she is very angry. She tries to hit me with a stick. I hide under the kitchen table. She pulls me out, calls me "a dirty little liar" and locks me down in the cellar. It is partly cement and partly dirt. It is dark and cold and damp. I am so scared. There are two shiny, glowing eyes staring at me. I think it is a cat. I am afraid to call my mom even though I am terrified of those glowing eyes. I stay very, very still and just wait.

Finally, after forever, Mom lets me out and tells me never to make up such terrible lies again. I promise. I know I can't tell her about Dad. I am so tired and my head aches. I walk through the fields and hide in the woods for awhile.

So there isn't any use in going to Mom for help. I'm always in trouble with her. No matter what I do, she is always mad with me. If my older sister spills her milk, it is an accident. If I spill my milk, it's on purpose, I'm told, and I get hit and yelled at.

I do very well in school but I am not allowed to tell anyone because my sister doesn't do as well. I am always being compared to her. She is very pretty and feminine and I am not. Mom constantly tells me I am messy, a slob, and ugly. "Why can't you be neat and clean like your sister?"

My brother is special, the only boy. Mom lets him do what he wants. He is pretty nice, though. Mom later has a baby girl. She is like a little doll and I like to take care of her.

We all work very hard at home. There is no running water, no bathroom in the house; there are only two bedrooms and curtains serve as doors in the bedrooms. Mom is always tired and angry. I am afraid of her. I would like her to love me. Most women frighten me. They always seem to be angry and yelling.

I continue to do well in school. I have lots of friends but I don't bring them home. I laugh a lot and joke. I am noisy and outgoing and I have a terrible temper. I behave mostly opposite to what my mom wants because she is always angry with me anyway. Why should I try to get her approval? I won't, so it doesn't matter. At least I get some kind of attention if I misbehave. But I still sometimes try. I really want her to love me.

memories are like a dark cloud growing inside me

My memories now are sometimes so vague and sometimes very vivid. With each remembrance comes a new feeling of being violated. I feel vulgar, unclean, and worthless. I have evil inside me and it is so powerful. I am afraid it can control me and cause me to harm the people I love. The evil is like a dark cloud that can grow when it is angry with me. It becomes so large that it fills my stomach, chest, and head. It whispers to me or gives me bad thoughts (thoughts of destroying myself, thoughts of its darkness consuming me).

The evil becomes very powerful and controlling when I remember the first time my father has intercourse with me. I am about ten years old or maybe eleven. We are alone in the house. My parents must have had another fight, probably about me. I have on a white blouse and a green skirt with a matching vest. I am standing in the living room holding a little purse that has been given to me as a gift on this day. My father calls me from his bedroom. I go to him and he hugs me. I tell him I am sorry, but I can't remember why. He helps me undress and I lie on the bed. It has a white bedspread. I am feeling tired. I don't want to do this tonight. I am thinking, "Please, Daddy, do this fast."

He lies beside me, rubbing my body. It is warm in the bedroom. He spreads my legs apart and probes with his fingers. I am clutching my hands against the pillows. He rubs his penis against me. I hate it. It is so ugly and it feels repulsive. Suddenly, he comes on top of me and pushes his penis inside me. I scream and his hand covers my mouth. He tells me he won't hurt me anymore, but he keeps pushing it inside me. I am crying and pleading, "Daddy, you're hurting me. Please stop! It hurts! Please stop!"

He stops. There is blood on the bedspread. I want to throw up. My dad gets a basin and washes me off a little. It helps the pain. He says, "Don't worry about the bedspread. I'll tell Mom I had a nosebleed."

I take my clothes and go to my room. I put on my pyjamas and crawl into bed and curl up in a ball. I feel so sick. My head is aching so badly and I have no safe place. I am so frightened and so ashamed. I hear my dad come into the room. I pretend I am asleep. He leaves.

Mom and the kids come home. I think Dad tells her I'm not feeling well because she comes into the room and asks me what's wrong. I tell her I have a bad headache. My mom begins to scream at me, "You had your eyes checked and there's nothing wrong with you. Stop this constant lying!" She pushes me against the window and strikes me around my head, over and over. I am so scared. There is no safe place. I can't get away. I'm trapped.

Later, when we are all in bed, (I share a bed with my older sister) my sister begins to wave her hands in front of my face. Hands frighten me. She knows this and keeps doing it. I can't call Mom; again, there is no safe place. I desperately need to hide.

The last time I remember being with my father sexually is when I am about twelve years old. Again, we are alone in the house. I remember being in his bedroom on their bed. I have no clothes on. My father is wearing a sleeveless undershirt and dark pants with suspenders, I think. He sits beside me on the bed and again there is the caressing and touching. He spreads my legs and probes with his fingers. He then lies on the bed beside me and continues to do this. I am thinking, "Please hurry. If you're going to put that thing inside me, please hurry and let it be over." He takes his penis out and rubs it against me. I hate it. It feels yucky. I am feeling anxious and afraid Mom will come home. I don't remember if he does have intercourse with me.

I hear the screen door slam. The next thing I know, Mom is in the bedroom. Dad is standing by the bed and I am still on the bed, naked. She starts yelling at me, "You filthy little tramp, you slut!" She leaves the room and I hear crashing like pots and pans falling. Then my mom comes back with the strap. It is all happening so fast. She is hitting me and calling me a filthy tramp and a slut. She hates me so much. I am crying and I can't get away.

Dad just stands there and lets her hurt me. Why doesn't he stop her? I didn't do anything wrong. I did what he wanted. Why doesn't he help me?

The next thing I remember is that I have a blanket wrapped around me. I am trying to walk to my bedroom. I am afraid I won't make it. My body is burning so badly and I am shaking. My sister and brother are sitting at the kitchen table staring at me. I feel so embarrassed and humiliated. They look like they hate me.

Later in bed, my sister tells me I do nothing but cause problems and upset everybody. She tells me that I don't belong there and she hates me for upsetting Mom. Then she tells me Mom let the cat in the house for the night. I am absolutely terrified. I am so afraid of cats. I don't know what to do. There is no place to go, no place to hide, no safe place anywhere. I remember nothing else, no further sex with my father. Perhaps it stopped there. I'm not sure.

drugs numb the pain

Later, I start getting violent headaches. When I am about seventeen, I start taking prescription drugs for these migraines. They help but I still need something else. Valium is prescribed. What a neat pill! I can relax for awhile and numb the pain. I can't figure out why I am so afraid all the time, but I find out that the medication not only fixes the migraine but also numbs the fear.

I begin abusing drugs when my first baby is twenty months old. Because I am experiencing severe emotional problems, I see a number of people in the psychiatric field, but my past is never examined. I am given tranquilizers and anti-depressants which only help on a short-term basis. By this time, I am chemically dependent. In order to feel good, I need to take more than is prescribed. This means I go without pills for a couple of days so that I have enough pills to make me feel completely numb. I keep this up for about nine years.

Alcohol also becomes a part of my life—a great stress-reliever. But the pills, especially the straight codeine tablets, are my main source of help for some sort of peace. I stop from time to time, but when I stop there is so much anger and fear inside me I feel crazy. I need pills so I will feel normal. During my second pregnancy I take my medication as prescribed by my doctor and make sure that what I do take is safe for my baby. I want to keep my baby safe.

After she is born, there is more pressure in my life and the fear and the panic grow. I begin to use codeine and alcohol again. I am afraid to talk to people. I feel inadequate. I feel that no one will pay attention to anything I have to say. If I am going to a parent/teacher interview for my son, I need to take codeine. It stimulates me and gives me confidence (false confidence). When I go to my son's soccer games or just out on the street where I might have to speak to a neighbour, I need to use pills or alcohol to give me a boost. I am so scared and I feel so crazy that I hide behind the drugs and alcohol. I don't want anyone to know about me. I think that I am safe and protected as long as I use drugs. I sometimes get so angry, I am afraid I will lose control. A drink, a dose of codeine, will snuff the bad feelings and I can get through another day.

I don't recognize that I have been abused

At this time, in therapy, I am asked if I was abused as a child. My mother physically and emotionally abused me but I always reply, "No," because I never had black eyes or broken bones. I don't think that what she did would count as abuse. I also successfully block out the relationship with my father and his friend. I know I have confused feelings about my childhood but I don't know what they are about. One therapist tells me, "You can't live in the past. Let it go and get on with your life." I know he is trying to help me in the best way possible and so are the many other therapists I see.

Eventually I learn that until the past has been taken care of, the present cannot get better. Although the therapists don't examine my childhood, I also might not be ready to expose myself. I am filled with shame and frightened to find out where that is coming from. At this time, I go to therapists with the idea that they can fix me the way a doctor can fix a broken arm. That gives them a lot of power. But over time, I learn a great deal from therapists. I learn that they don't know everything, that they make mistakes and most of the ones with whom I have been connected don't want to be in control. They are there to guide me, support me and be with me in my torment and in my healing. They cannot make me all better. That is for me to do. They give me tools to do the work and all the encouragement I need.

I am grateful to the doctor who cares enough about me to make sure that I get the help I need. He makes all the arrangements for me to get started along a path that leads to my entering a chemical dependency program. It takes a long time to come to terms with what I did to myself and a long time to lose the need to be taking something.

remembering allows me to start to make sense of my life

After not using chemicals for almost three years and while seeing an excellent therapist from a chemical dependency program, I start to remember the incest and begin to tell him about it. Up until now, I do not know anyone whom I trust and with whom I feel really safe. I have no idea that my using has anything to do with my past. One of the feelings that comes with the remembering is a huge sense of relief. I am not crazy. I am not an emotional cripple. I have a real reason for having these powerful feelings— the devastation, anger, depression, the evil feeling. I do not need to hide behind chemicals anymore. I am not sick, just hurting a lot and I can overcome that hurt. I can start to make sense out of my life.

it is a great relief to meet other sexual abuse survivors

After the memories start to come, my therapist at the chemical dependency program sends me to the Women's Post Treatment Centre where women who were sexually abused as children are given counselling. It is scary to go but it is the best thing I could have done for myself. One of the major feelings that I have to overcome about the incest is the fear that everyone can tell what has happened to me just by looking at me, especially if we make eye contact. I keep my head down a lot because of that fear. It is a big relief for me when I meet other incest survivors and find that I can't tell just by looking at them or in general conversation that anything has ever happened. They look very "normal," as do I.

I call the cloud inside me "the evil"

However, I have a problem that is never discussed in depth with the other women. I feel I have an evil entity inside myself. Stopping the use of chemicals has brought so much pain that I can't block the evil inside me anymore. As far as I recall the evil has been a part of me for the past several years. I always feel that people can tell it is there and that it can provoke them to hurt me and me to hurt them. Therefore, I think I deserve to be hurt. It is like a cloud (probably male) in my abdomen, that grows when I am angry and fills my chest and head. I often feel possessed, sometimes feeling that the evil is not something separate from me—it is me.

For several years I am aware of the cloud inside me. I am afraid of it and I feel tormented. Often the cloud seems to be taunting me—pushing me to hurt others but instead I inflict the hurt on me. I am afraid to speak of it, terrified of its rage, terrified of what it might make me do. But, I decide to take the risk. I talk about it with my therapists. I think I can do this because when I am with them I feel safe and protected. With their help, I am able to identify it. I call it "the evil". It is dark and sinister. "The evil" fits. Through my therapy, I find ways of dealing with "the evil."

To make the cloud ("the evil") inside of me small, I imagine a steel rim around the cloud pulling it tighter and tighter until the cloud is very small. I am afraid to get rid of it entirely, perhaps because I have felt its presence for so long and there will be an emptiness that I won't know how to fill.

I also visualize inside me a soft, white light like the light of God or a Higher Power that is pure and good and more powerful than anything evil. With the help of one of my therapists, I learn how to bring this light inside my body. With a great deal of concentration, I bring the light in through the top of my head and draw it slowly through my body so it can clean my spirit. Each time the cloud comes inside me, I try to do this. Sometimes it is very effective. As I become well, there is less need to do this. The cloud remains very small and sometimes I feel it is gone altogether.

the evil moves outside and hovers over

In talking with my therapists from the Women's Post Treatment Centre and from the Chemical Dependency Unit about the evil, I begin to experience another phenomenon. I feel a shadow hover over me as I lie in bed. I can feel it lie on top of me so that I find it hard to breathe. Sometimes I feel it having intercourse with me. It whispers angrily that I am a slut, filth, garbage! I can even feel its presence in the shower or just behind me as I work about the house. I feel quite alone, very weird and crazy again. The fear is tumbling around inside of me. I feel that I can't share this, but I do. I am assured that this experience is "normal" for someone who has had an abusive childhood. I am given material to read which helps me realize I am not alone and not crazy. I begin to talk about the problem with other sexual abuse survivors and find several who experience similar disturbances.

With the shadow outside of me, I have to be very firm. It does not like rituals or Christian symbols. The purity and strength of a Higher Power scare the shadow so I wear a cross all the time for months for protection and keep a Bible on my night table beside my bed. I also draw an imaginary circle around my bed every night. The shadow is not allowed inside the circle.

There is a lot of pain and fear involved in doing this. The shadow lets me know he is dying and I feel as if I might die as well. I am exhausted, but gradually I become more energetic. As I become less fearful and vulnerable and feel stronger, the presence of the shadow becomes weaker.

I learn not all women are hurtful

These are enormous risks for me to take but I have a great deal of support. My therapists from the chemical dependency program and from Women's Post Treatment Centre are caring and understanding. In coming to know the gentle women who are my therapists in the sexual abuse program, I lose some of my fear of women and learn that not all women (especially those in an authority position) are angry and hurtful. They also help me to believe that what I am remembering is true and help build my self-esteem by offering me volunteer opportunities. I use the tools they teach me to use, such as an "anger journal" and a "fear journal" in which I pour out in writing my fear and anger and learn to accept it. To survive, I often have to stay in the feeling, experiencing it fully, and so eventually working through it. To cope with the tough stuff—dealing with all these scary emotions—I do physical things such as bike riding, swimming, and hard work around the house.

Working through this and trying to build some sort of value for myself, some sense of worth, is the hardest, scariest thing I have ever done. I feel angry and resentful that I have to use a large part of my life to do this while my "good, upstanding parents" don't have to do anything. There is a great deal of rage with which I haven't begun to deal. Through my nervous breakdown and my suicide attempts, my parents never say a word to help me, even though they are asked about any childhood trauma I may have had. I guess they want to save themselves. I have been used and abused, and even now they refuse to admit anything ever happened. I don't think they love me now or ever loved me the way parents truly love their child. Our relationship is purely superficial. They know I remember but their denial is very strong. I think that I will have to learn to live with and accept their denial.

I work hard to build a sense of self-worth in the face of my parents' denial of what happened to me

I love my own children very much and feel that I am an okay mom. I am married to a quiet, gentle man. My marriage is not ideal. The incest has had an impact on our relationship that requires a great deal of work from my husband and myself. I often feel that I am working alone in our relationship (as if the incest is my problem and so I should take care of it). But we have had couple counselling and that is something that I think has been necessary and helpful to us. Our sexual relationship has suffered and I need to learn to set boundaries and respect my rights so that eventually I can become comfortable with sexual intimacy. I enjoy being a mom and a homemaker and doing crafts like knitting, crocheting and needlepoint. I do some volunteer work and teach Sunday School. I am also starting to work part-time outside of my home. I am still more comfortable and find it easier to communicate with children than with adults.

being part of a self-help support group creates a safe place where I can give and receive support

Several women, including myself, expressed a need for a self-help support group. With help and resources from the Women's Post Treatment Centre, we established such a group. It is hard work, but I think it is also an important part of our healing. In laying the groundwork for this group—setting up guidelines and rules—we are finally doing something for ourselves. We are learning to take care of our own needs. I am developing a strong bond with these women and the support is always there. Being a group member gives me a sense of fitting in, of belonging. I finally have a safe place to be after so many years of having no safe place.

I still have a lot of inner fear of what I will become now that I am no longer an incest "victim," but there is also a feeling that says, "I'm alive and kicking." Dealing with the incest through a group also gives me the opportunity to help other women, so something positive is coming out of something so overwhelmingly negative.

There is fear and insecurity in my life still; but each time I tell more of this terrible "secret," I think I move forward a little. I cannot let the terror freeze me. It is often very powerful, but the support from other survivors and my therapists helps me to feel safe and I can take another step. I still need lots of love and reassurance but I am also more independent and my thoughts and my feelings are becoming mine, not my parents'.

I listen to the child who is inside me and needs to be heard. I listen to the adult inside me who seems strong and wise, and I listen to the "nameless someone" inside me who is trapped by terror, pain and grief. I feel like my body is a house for all these people and I'm not sure who I am. When I listen closely to what they are saying, I begin to disappear, but if I can stay connected to them and listen, I know that they are the ones I need to hear. They are the ones who are going to give me my identity and help push the old, dangerous, harmful messages away. I know this is beginning to happen because I allow these three people to live in my body. I can hear them speak and if I want to, I can listen and learn and grow up and be one whole person who is "someone."

a dialogue with hope

The last thing I want to speak of is hope. I spent a great deal of time thinking about this and wondering if I really do have hope. In a workshop I attended, we were told of how one person learned about the feeling of joy by having a dialogue with it. It is wonderful and I decided to try to find out what hope is for me, or if I even have hope, by doing the same thing. This is what happened:

ME: Do I have hope?
HOPE: Yes, I am here. I am how you get through each day and each night.
ME: I think of you as looking forward with anticipation and excitement. I don't feel that. I think you are not in me.
HOPE: Look into yourself. Determine your own definition of me. Give your-self a new message of who I am.
ME: I feel like I am walking through my life on the narrow railing of a bridge high above the ground. If I fall, my life will be over. I am really scared. I think the narrow railing is the risks I must take in therapy, in sharing my experiences about the abuse and what I am like be-cause of it. The narrow railing is the risks I take in reaching out to people, in making decisions, in getting through each day. I have lost my balance on the railing but I have not fallen and died. Know-ing that, I must trust in what I have done to heal myself and con-tinue to move forward on the narrow railing. Trusting in what I have done helps me to take the next step. I think that is my "hope."
HOPE: You have looked into your heart and you have found me. I am with you all the time. When you make it through a whole day and when you make it through a tormented night, it is because I am there.
ME: I am glad that I took this time to find you. It is good to know you are in-side of me. I feel safer knowing you are with me.
                                                                                                    "

♦

Megan is forty-one years old, married, and has two children. "I have a nice house in a nice neighbourhood. My parents were respected members of the community. When I began to remember the incest, I did not want to believe it. I thought: my parents couldn't be like that!

"At the time I write this, I have been dealing with the memories of incest and abuse for four years. I no longer deny that it happened. I move on in spite of it.

"I live with an incredible sadness that I think will never leave. I survived sexual abuse as a child and I am surviving the memory of it as an adult. I want to be known as more than a survivor. I want to be recognized as a 'real' person—as 'a someone.' "

ritual abuse

Gaia

"
I am a ritual abuse survivor. The abuse took place when I was between three and seven years old. In 1968, my mom saved her three children from the ritual abuse by bringing us to Manitoba.

When I was five I was a satanic bride. My dad first penetrated me when I was three. I don't know how young I was when I was performing oral sex, but I believe that I was less than a year old. I was brutally beaten with a piece of bamboo from a very early age, burned with cigarettes under my arms and on my feet, and gang-banged by the cult members at the age of five. (I wrote that numb.) I was a murderess—no, a killing machine—for the cult when I was five.

I was a very quiet, "good" child (too good). When my dad beat me or raped me I was silent. It wasn't until I got into therapy that I was able to cry away the tears that had been suppressed for over twenty years. The medical profession believes that I'm manic-depressive because I talk too much. I know that I'm simply making up for all those years that I was silenced.

My dad is/was a satanic high priest. I don't know if he's still involved with the cult, but I do know that after I confronted him by letter last year about the incest, he not only told me that I had a vivid imagination, but that I should consider not seeing my therapist anymore. One month later, he sent a copy of his will to both my mom and my brother. That was his way of validating his "love" for his children, I suppose. My dad and I haven't corresponded since that time.

The memories lay well-hidden until I went to see a psychologist because I'd quit smoking for three months and had gained fifteen pounds. I still smoke—three-and-a-half years later. Dealing with flashbacks, nightmares and deeply suppressed feelings is the main issue now. Most important, I'm unravelling my concept that love equals pain, or that when I'm feeling safe, danger will ensue. I'm currently working with a counsellor who specializes in ritual abuse. I'm also seeing a psychiatric resident and I'm in the process of educating him about the healing process.

I am still healing, and have learned through my personal experiences that this process just can't be rushed.

releasing memories through music and writing

I believe the healing process first began when I was fourteen. I overdosed on twenty-one Midol after listening to a Simon and Garfunkel tune, *The Sound of Silence*, during an English class. Later, in therapy, I connected the song to what was playing in the car one evening when my dad was molesting me. I was five. I didn't understand the connection at fourteen, but something valuable came out of it. I began to write. I wrote poetry as a coping mechanism for many years, but kept my writings from the eyes of everyone, except myself.

Through my therapy, feelings arose in this order: fear, anger, hurt, love. Then I began to feel the memories in the form of flashbacks.

I'd never had a panic attack before I entered into the healing process. Strangely, during these attacks, I don't feel fear at all. I go numb and feel like I can't breathe. These attacks still haunt me once in a while. I've programmed myself to think, "I am safe, it's 1990, and it happened over twenty years ago."

Now I get surges of fear once in a while, but they don't last long, and they are usually clues to a brand new memory underway. It's still a mystery to me how the mind stores the memories in our bodies. But I do know my right knee hurts before a memory is underway. Some survivors get headaches, nauseated, or some other psychosomatic trigger before a new memory is underway.

New memories are usually released through writing. My whole body goes numb, and I enter what I call a "trance" state. The details are incredible. Sometimes the colours of the shoes I was wearing, or the smells that were in the air, come out on the paper.

I would advise any survivor to write. I believe that the only possible way for the abuse cycle to stop is through the healing process, not through numbing our bodies with prescription or non-prescription drugs.

anger started to come out

My anger started to come forth about two years ago. It was so intense that I'd be walking down the street visualizing myself pounding perpetrators' penises and breasts onto the neighbourhood trees. I remember telling my therapist to put me into the psych ward for a while, but he kept saying how my thoughts weren't hurting anyone. I did survive. I just kept writing and writing.   It was the anger that eventually led me to confront my dad about the incest. This was before any of the ritual stuff came out. I believed somehow that if I wrote him and went through the motions of forgiving him on paper, then the anger would end. It helped a little, but I hadn't forgiven him.

At the time my whole upper trunk was covered in a rash. The rash was by body's way of helping me to release the anger, I think. Anyway, the rash resolved itself a month after I wrote him and only lasted for a total of two months.

My dad denies everything and I suspect he always will, but after I held a cleansing ritual this past month to forgive myself, that forgiveness toward him finally arrived. I recognize that the anger and the fear may interfere with this time and time again, but it was through forgiving myself that I was able to gain some insight into the abusers of the world. I acknowledged all of the perpetrators' inner fears, anger and emotional pain. This is what I believe causes not only ritual abuse to exist, but also the abuse cycle in general.

Women's spirituality has been a great help to me through this journey. I find the rituals both cleansing and healing, perhaps because, to me, they express the exact opposite of what satanism is all about.

when my boyfriend wanted to get closer I thought he was a satanist

Intimacy, especially with men, has always been an issue with me. That's how my most recent breakdown began. I ended up at a women's shelter, really delusional. I thought that my lover was a satanist and that he was out to make a human sacrifice out of me if I didn't do as he wanted (marry him). I also had telepathy with him, or so I thought, which was how I got the information that he wanted to marry me. The experience of telepathy began after he and I had a fight. He had been trying to get closer to me and I wanted to run like hell. That's what my delusions were all about. I wanted to trust him.

In the week that followed, I kept feeling my dad's stick beating me, and the cigarette burns. I had a whole week of vivid body memories and was absolutely terrified of my boyfriend—who is, in fact, a real sweetheart. In Freudian terms, this is called transference.

I went through six weeks of pure hell before my mom finally had me committed to the psych ward.

But the delusions were actually helpful to me. I believe that delusions can be. I was trying to make myself feel safer, so that I could trust my gentle boyfriend. In my delusions, he started out as a satanist and ended up the reincarnation of Jesus. My therapist became the reincarnation of Noah, and all the satanists, including my dad, became healers.

It's over, and I now feel very safe, and I am delusion-free.

ritual abuse was called fashionable

The most difficult thing about being on the psych unit was my complete loss of freedom, and the overwhelming sense of powerlessness, in a system that hasn't yet understood the healing process. Not once was I offered therapy for the ritual abuse, and I was actually told that it was "fashionable." I was so over-medicated that I couldn't write, had difficulty speaking, walking, sleeping. Even curling my hair with a curling-iron took great concentration and effort, although I had been delusion-free three days after admission.

I felt like I wasn't being heard for the entire seven weeks. If I said I felt depressed, I was told that it simply couldn't be true. It wasn't until I became extremely suicidal that I was believed. It was then that they discontinued the drug that was causing the depression. I was given the antidote for the drug they had me on, and felt two hundred percent better within half an hour. Manic-depressive indeed! I am a survivor!

When I consider the three years of panic attacks, the breakdown, vivid flashbacks, memories that appear to have come out of some deep level within my unconscious, and the nightmares of rape and physical attack—all of which are a result of the violence I experienced during the first seven years of my life—I know I've come a long way. But there are still days, I have to admit, that I question why I ever delved into my past. This is particularly true since the delusional episode, and my confrontation with the medical system, where, on the whole, there is gross error and an overwhelming depth of misunderstanding about the healing process.

post-traumatic stress disorder

Survivors of ritual abuse are suffering from post-traumatic stress disorder, much like the survivors of the Holocaust, Vietnam, or any other type of war. Survivors are not crazy or manic-depressive, they are working out the brutal impact of past experience on their minds and bodies.

Survivors are human beings who are recovering from the trauma they once blocked from their conscious awareness—trauma they blocked in order to survive. Once their previous coping mechanisms become inadequate, or they begin to feel really safe in this world, the memories begin to surface.

One of the best gifts that I've received through this process is my ability to hug my male friends with a sense of warmth and safety. And I am now freer in every aspect of my life. I now say what I mean to say, what I believe needs to be said.

I've learned through the healing process that I've always intellectualized caring. I believed that love was an action, but now I know that love is a very safe, warm feeling that I feel inside. I've learned that love encompasses understanding, empathy, safety and caring that comes from the heart. Caring isn't merely an action to me anymore.

I spoke about my hospitalization as a very negative experience. It wasn't all negative, and the staff were trying to help me in the best way they could. My stay in hospital helped me to realize that I am actually very lovable.

I have a message to all those in the medical profession: please listen carefully to what survivors have to say. Perhaps, then, we can all learn from one another. Above all else, survivors, I believe, need to be listened to with a supportive, non-judgemental ear.

"

♦

Gaia is twenty-nine-year-old single parent who is an R.N. Her daughter, now seven, had been sexually abused by four men, including the natural father. That man also involved his daughter in child pornography. The other three men were a landlord, a friend and a babysitter. Gaia spent the two years before her breakdown studying for a B.A. in psychology. She is currently working as a nurse again.

my body—preparing for a memory

Phoenix

"

When a new memory is coming to me I get signals from my body. It usually involves a part of my body hurting for no reason that I can relate to the present. The reasons for the pain are related to past ages and experiences.

For example, memories from when I was eight years old and was injured in an assault always begin in my right shoulder. Memories of teenage abuse experiences are generally foreshadowed by pain in my thighs. I also get rashes and stomach aches.

These kinds of things go on for two or three days and thus I know that more memory is coming. I begin having insomnia and become more and more anxious, tired and insecure. I usually call my counsellor and set up an appointment for afterwards. The memory usually first comes in my sleep, and usually in a dream.

Afterwards I cry a lot and deal with what I have learned, by writing and sorting it out partly on my own and partly with my counsellor. When a memory comes more and more fully, I feel very scared and small. Something that helped me in my healing was my pillow nest. I found I needed a place within my house that was just for me. This was my bed. I made lots of pillows and one special pillow was two feet by five feet in size. When I was dealing with the darkest of my memories I would curl up inside all my pillows, and I would hold and hug my big pillow. It was a womb—my warm, safe, protected place; soft surroundings in which I could cry, thrash, rage and bury myself with my deepest pain. The tactile sensations of softness all around me made the pain, even the deepest pain, easier to withstand. I saw myself as a small furry animal—such as a fox—who had been badly hurt. I thought of a fox because a fox has sharp teeth and I "bite" when I am hurt. And, like a fox, I hide in my cave when hurting. Looking back on it, the pillow nest was the womb and pain was the birthing of myself.

I still take time for myself to read, muse and write in the comfort of my nest. I even had a painting done of me—the painter painted pillows all around me. He said it just seemed like me.

"

◆

Phoenix is now thirty-four. She was thirty when the memories could be denied no longer. In her past was a nightmare of ten years of abuse. "There were five different male abusers and a satanic ritual. Only luck can be credited with my survival," she says. "It took two and a half years of therapy for me to learn to cope with these memories. I thought I would cry a river, a real river. And the emotional pain was so deep it caused physical pain. When I was my most fragile I had several real stabilizers in my life: my therapist, a strong, determined woman; and a husband whose love was abiding and whose pain at watching someone he loved cry was almost equal to my own. He was a victim of the abuse in my life too.

"The crying has turned to laughter. A job and hobbies, mostly books, take up my time. I'm a new woman now. It's wonderful."

leaving my body

Moira

"

I have often had to ask people to repeat questions because I haven't been there.

I had been doing a lot of thinking about how I left my body, where I went, and how I returned. One day in a counselling session, we were discussing, quite intensely, my "leaving my body." I saw my counsellor looking quizzically at me—she was waiting for an answer.

At that point I saw my hands on my knees and could feel myself returning. I had a "pins and needles" sensation throughout my body right down to those finger tips on my knees.

Later in that session I left my body again. I had a sensation like being on a swing and being pulled backwards and upwards. Returning to my body, I experienced a forward-swinging sensation, almost as if my feet were going up in the way they do on a swing.

"

♦

Moira is separated and has three sons. She works as a registered nurse. "I was in and out of A.A. for three years before I got into counselling for abuse and addiction issues. Before I got counselling for the terrible abuse I'd suffered as a child, I couldn't maintain any length of sobriety. I would get six months of sobriety, then eleven months and then I would drink again.

"Two-and-a-half years ago I got into counselling and I now have three-and-a-half years of sobriety. The first two years of counselling were hell, but this past year has been just wonderful. For fifty years I felt like I was in jail, doing nothing but hard labour. Now I'm living and it's a good feeling. I am being recognized at work and in my personal life. I have worked hard all my life and still am, but now it feels good.

"I have so much gratitude to my higher power, A.A. and the WPTC. I needed all of them."

— Moira

GROWING UP
BECOMING A LADY —

FRONT	BACK

WELTS

LEARNING TO CURTSY

LEARNING TO HIDE PAIN — FEAR — ANGER — RAGE + LONGING TO BE WANTED NEEDED, LOVED

— Moira

journalling and drawing for self-healing

Brenda Lynn

"
As I look back at my notebooks filled with thoughts and drawings from the past several years, I am amazed to see so many penises hidden there. I know that children who have been sexually abused often draw penises in their pictures, but I'm a grown woman. I look at a rock I drew a year ago and it looks suspiciously like a penis. I used to have dreams of mushrooms when I was a child and when I look at my drawings of mushrooms in my books, again they are penises. I am looking at my own symbols for men and my abuse and I didn't even know that I was drawing them.

When I was little I was always a "good" girl and I used the correct colours and always coloured inside the lines. I never allowed myself a spark of creativity. My "little girl" has been left behind somewhere, but I'm now finding her. I now allow myself to write what I really feel and draw what I want. I feel this incredible need to just put it down on paper so it will be more real. All my hate, anger, love, jealousy, fear, joy. I put it down on paper now. It's like having my own private therapist available twenty-four hours a day.

I began by taking courses in journalling, and reading books. One series of books I found to be really helpful is by Lucia Capacchione. She combines writing and drawing and makes you feel that you can do this too. Looking at the pictures in her books, I realized that I didn't need to be an artist or even be able to draw. All I needed was the desire to express myself. I drew stick people, slashes of colour, hate words, whatever I was feeling.

It is almost as if when I draw or write, the emotions start healing. I don't always feel the need to analyze the drawings. Often, just the physical act of drawing an emotion in a particular colour starts to lift the feelings of depression or sadness. I begin by sitting quietly and by meditating or listening to music, then I just allow it to flow out of me as I pick up the pen.

I often write and draw my dreams. They seem to have a greater wisdom that I can call upon. The physical act of getting it on paper helps me to remember the dream and make it real. Otherwise, the thought or dream just seems to evaporate.

I often have a dialogue with people or parts of my body through writing. I get quiet and then write with one hand to this other object or person and get answers from them with my other hand. It just seems to come. I don't force it or think about it. It just seems to be there and I write it down. Once, when talking to my body, I asked it why I sometimes gag when brushing my teeth. My body replied that my father had put his penis in my mouth, and brushing my teeth brought up the feelings. This was the first time I realized that this had happened. After that I filled my pages with black and red slashes filled with anger and hate and many pages of dialogue with my "little girl." The act seemed so real because I had it on paper—it seemed so fuzzy and imaginary otherwise. Someday, I may even have the courage to carry on a dialogue with my father in my pages.

I look back and see a pattern to my journalling. I don't see it when I'm actually doing it. I see an emotion, a memory or a situation and I write or draw about it. Then there is a series of pages dealing with the feelings and memories that come up. Finally, there is a release and sense of joy. This cycle can take weeks or hours, and it happens at its own pace. I can feel blocked emotions being released like layers of an onion. It's good to look back and see the times of joy, love and happiness because that is also part of my life.

I just put down what I want. It is private, no one else sees my books. I might just list what happened to me today or quote something important from a book or talk to a person who is dead. It's my own.

People use these techniques to heal from physical illnesses. Scientists have proven that by drawing or writing feelings, chemicals are released in the body that help to heal the immune system. I know that my emotions are being healed by this process. I may not remember much of my past, but I have strong emotions and when I journal I find out who I am. It's my path to healing.

"

◆

Brenda Lynn is a forty-year-old woman who works as a professional in the helping field. "I have spent most of my life helping other people with their problems," she says. "However, for the past several years, including a year-and-a-half in therapy, I have changed my focus to try to heal from an abusive childhood. I was adopted and I never felt I belonged in my family. This is a theme that has been repeated throughout my life.

"Now I am trying to find love and peace within myself. I use journalling to keep growing into my self-love, and I send love to each of you on your path."

a letter to myself as a child

Marie

"*D*earMarie,

I wish I could have been there thirty-two years ago. You needed to be told it wasn't your fault. I would have held you and told you how strong and courageous you were to tell Mom. You were only eight—just a little girl. When I look at your picture now, I see an innocent child wanting to be loved and cuddled.

You felt lost in the maze of a huge family. Mom was constantly trying to keep up with meals, laundry and diapers. Dad was unable to show any affection. There never were special times with Mom and Dad when you felt you were important.

There was no sense of being an individual; no privacy. You trusted all grown-ups and your older brother John was a grown-up in your eyes— much bigger and very much respected and in charge.

He may have only been sixteen but he knew he was doing wrong.

Marie, you, on the other hand, were very confused: "It is wrong but John thinks I'm special ... It's wrong. Everyone says how good John is but this is wrong. It feels good to be cuddled; it feels good to be special ... but this is wrong." Your conclusion, little Marie, was: "Then I must be bad."

Marie, how could a little eight-year-old understand? No one ever explained it to you! Then you realized that it was happening to Peggy as well. You felt responsible because you were "older" and should have taken care of your little sister. My child, how could you have been responsible for Peggy? You were only eight!

You were, in fact, a very strong little girl. You risked a lot by telling Mom. And she listened attentively as you told her how your big brother "put his front bum into my front bum." She stood there, seemingly miles away from you and listened. She said she would make sure it didn't happen again and it didn't. She didn't blame you or accuse you. She didn't make you feel that she didn't believe you.

Mom did the best she could, but how much better things would have been had she spent some time with you afterwards, just cuddling and letting you know that you did the right thing—that you weren't to blame, you weren't bad. So many of your thoughts could have been positive instead of negative. You would not have felt shame and guilt when John joined the church and left home. You wouldn't have felt shame when he returned. If only someone had told you, you were not to blame, you wouldn't have felt such discomfort in his presence—always seeing him as the favourite, the good one, the man of God.

No one told you that you were a little girl who placed innocent trust in a big brother. That brother took advantage of you. He took away your childhood, your childish games and gave you a lifetime of guilt and shame. You wanted love and attention and to just feel special, important. He gave you hopelessness, intimidation, fear of men, self-hatred, worthlessness.

When you grew up these feelings crowded your mind in subtle ways but were there none the less. Remember your self-destructive behaviour? Oh you didn't think it was so destructive then. You thought Ed was the answer. Finally someone loved you. His drinking and drug abuse didn't cause you any great concern until after the marriage. Ed said it was your fault he drank and ran around. Of course you believed him. What else would you expect? How could you ever think that you could be loved and happy? You saw yourself as insignificant and unloved. Even God had abandoned you. Valium helped. For awhile.

My dear little girl, you were at rock bottom. You saw nothing good, nothing beautiful in yourself. But the strength and courage were still there. It was part of you from years gone by and it resurfaced at that point. You took your children and left an abusive, alcoholic husband.

Little one, I wish I could go back and undo the pain of the past. It isn't possible. Please feel how proud I am of you. You have a rare strength! And see what you've been able to do with your life. You are a functioning and valuable contributor to society—a professional now, helping others. In times of difficulty you come through because you remember a greater hurdle from childhood. Your pessimism almost consumed you once but your basic strength came through as it always does in the long run. No, I cannot undo the pain, but together we can allow that pain to move us toward change and growth. We will embrace the pain, go through it and gradually release it. Then we will experience its healing salve. Yesterday's only value is in helping us to live a better today. Learn and grow from yesterday—hope in tomorrow but, Marie, live only one day at a time.

I love you, //

Your "Adult" Self.

Marie works full time as a health care professional. She remarried and has two teenaged children. "Healing started for me after attending a group for the separated and divorced," she says. "I am currently in a Twelve Step Program."

dear mom

Misty

"*D*ear Mom,

I am writing to you now because I didn't have the courage to talk to you before. Also because I didn't know what was causing so many of my problems. I love you and miss you so much. I wish we had been closer, and I'd been sure I could talk to you about anything when I was young.

I am sure you know how much I hated Dad—his drinking and the way he used to hit you when he had been drinking. I was always scared of him, yet there were times when I wanted to be able to kill him, so he wouldn't hurt you ever again. I used to think we would be better off if he was dead. Now he is dead and I miss him too, in a way, but it's you I would like to be able to see again. We could have fun and talk like we should have when I was too scared and ashamed to talk to anyone.

Mom, I hate to have to tell you this because I don't want to hurt you, but your favourite son abused me when I was about six or seven. I used to be scared to go to bed at night because I didn't want him to come into my room after he thought I was asleep. I hated the sound of those footsteps coming down the hall to my room. I'd pull the covers over my head and pretend to be asleep. He'd come in and reach under the covers to touch, feel, and press the private parts of my body. I was always so scared, and if he realized I wasn't sleeping he would tell me to be quiet and not to say anything to anybody. I would send my mind off riding my horse most of the time just so I wouldn't have to think about what he was doing to me. I didn't really know what it was all about, I just knew it was wrong.

Another thing I never told you about, and should have, was my best friend's dad. He abused me from the time I was six or seven until I was about thirteen.

He did the kinds of things little kids enjoy doing: playing hide and seek, tag, swimming, hiking, camping and—best of all for me—riding horseback. He did all kinds of dumb things with us that Dad would never have considered doing. The only time Dad would fool around with us was when he had been drinking, if he didn't get in the mood to fight with you first.

I don't know if my abuser's family had any idea about what was going on with us. It's hard for me to think back now and believe they didn't know. He seemed so open about it: touching and feeling me while we were supposed to be swimming. You know where we used to swim, so you know why I'm wondering how the abuse could have occurred, and nobody known about it. Another place was on their living room couch, when we would all pile on him to watch TV. It seemed that even when I started out on top of the pile, soon he had shifted us around until I was against him, and the touching would start again. How can stuff like that go on in your own living room with your wife and kids there and nobody see that something is wrong?

There were also our camping trips when we'd spend the weekends out at the lake. It didn't matter whether we'd sleep in a tent or all outside under the blankets, it seemed that I would always go to bed as far away from him as possible, but when I woke up (because of the touching, again) he was beside me. His touching me was bad enough, but he also started to make me touch him.

Mom, I started to love and hate him at the same time. I loved him because he did enjoyable things with us that Dad never did, and I hated him for the abuse he put me through. I loved him for his friendship, and the way he made me feel important and wanted—I guess just real attention that I never received from Dad. I also hated him because I trusted him and he violated that trust and me. I also hated myself during this time because, as I got a little older, I sometimes enjoyed being touched and almost looked forward to it. I would then feel guilty, dirty and disgusted with myself for enjoying what was being done to me.

Mom, I really wish that I could have come to you and told you about what was happening. I am sure you would have believed me and understood what I was being put through by him. I wasn't so sure you would have believed me about my brother but, looking back now, I know I should have talked to you about it anyway. I want to tell you, too, what these incidents have done to my life since I was a child.

You wouldn't have approved that I had sex with guys I dated, although I am sure you suspected that something was happening. I have since found that that's all it was—just sex. I hated the sex part of dating but it seemed that each guy expected it and since I didn't have much of an opinion of myself—because of what had been done to me as a child—I thought I could hold the guy if I had sex with him. They were only out to satisfy themselves and didn't care how I felt so, of course, my opinion of myself dropped even lower. I felt I wasn't good enough for anybody and that's why none of the relationships lasted for any length of time, except one.

You know who I mean and I don't even know why it went on for as long as it did. We seemed to fight almost constantly about sex and other things but I guess he didn't want to lose his regular supply. He was another one that I both loved and hated. I loved him for some of the things that were very important to both of us, like our love for horses, but hated him because he wanted sex at the strangest times and places. He called it making love but I now know that all he wanted was relief. I know that sounds like going to the bathroom but that's how I felt about it. He never seemed to care about my feelings, only getting relief for himself. I sure know now the difference between making love and just having sex.

I think another reason I allowed those guys to have sex with me was to get even with Dad because I knew how mad it would have made him, if he had known. He probably would have beat me for it, or beat you for raising a slut of a daughter. I guess I didn't think about him possibly taking it out on you, or I wouldn't have done it. I sure didn't want him to hurt you anymore than he already had. I think I just hated him so much that I wanted to hurt him in any way that I could, even if I hurt myself in the process.

Then I met the guy that I knew I was going to marry. He was so much more considerate than any of the others. We've had some pretty tough times throughout our marriage, as far as our sex life is concerned. I love him so much and he has been so kind and understanding, even though he didn't know why I usually cried when we made love. He would think he had hurt me and apologize for whatever he had done wrong even though he had done nothing wrong—it was just me—and we'd end up crying together.

During fifteen years of marriage, I've never had an orgasm. I didn't know what an orgasm was but I knew there was something wrong with me. My husband also thought that he was doing something wrong that prevented me from having the orgasm. I feel so sorry for the things that he's been through during our marriage. I even went so far as to have a couple of affairs to see if my husband and I were doing something wrong. They had the same results. I then had something else to feel guilty about and hate myself for. I've told my husband about the affairs and why I did it. He understands completely.

When I remembered the abuse, after I began to see a psychiatrist, I told my husband everything that had happened to me and he has stood with me through it all. Our love life has improved since I told him the whole story— so much so, that I find it hard to believe. God, if I had known years ago what the problem was, we wouldn't have had to go through all those years of torment trying to figure out what we were doing wrong. It's terrible what the years have built up; it's terrible what guilt, hate and low self-esteem can do to a person.

Since I've been in counselling I've learned a lot about myself, the things that happened to me as a child, and why I still feel the way I do—about Dad especially. I sincerely hope that all women who have ever been through any type of abuse will go for counselling and get the help they need—so they can better understand their situation, how they have learned to survive, and what they can now do to change their way of thinking and dealing with the past. And so they can learn how to get on with their lives and not always have the big black cloud of guilt, hate and dislike for themselves and others, hanging over their heads.

I don't know how my husband and I would have made out if I hadn't got help when I did and learned how to deal with my past. I had seriously considered suicide at different times in my life and didn't know why. Thank God I received help when I did because I can truthfully say that suicidal thoughts are now a thing of the past.

Mom, there is another thing that I really want to be able to do, and that is to be able to think about Dad without all the hate and anger that I have inside for him. I know he was behind a lot of the problems that I had because he didn't fill the father role the way he should have. I want to be able to think about Dad differently. If there is any way I can do this I sure hope I can find it. I am tired of thinking about him and constantly talking about all the things I hate about him. I hope this can soon be resolved so I can carry on with a normal life.

Like I said before, Mom, I wish you were here so I could tell you this face to face. I love you so much, and really wish I had told you more when you were here.

All my love forever,
your loving daughter,

Misty

"

dear dad

Jeannine

I wrote the following letter prior to finally visiting my father's grave for the first time. At this point I'd already been in therapy for ten months, following a severe depression. At the onset of my illness I was not aware of my denial of my past abuse. I'd blocked it from my mind. I also had not accepted my father's death. These were my words of goodbye to him and my past.

"*D*ear Dad,

It's been ten years since you died. It is only now that I accept I'll never see or fear you again. Oh how I feared you!

You were my father and you hurt me. Even now, at the age of thirty-five, I still hurt. What we called our family was a far cry from a normal family. We didn't have a chance with you. Your drinking caused me shame. Because of your alcohol we were always moving with no warning. Even today I can't make good friends because I fear losing them as I always did in the past. I have no place to call home!

With the drinking came the abuse. You tortured my mind and my emotions. In time I lost my dignity and self-respect. I remember so well how you called me stupid, lazy, ugly, and good-for-nothing. I tried so hard to please you, yet I was never good enough. All I wanted was to be loved—unconditionally.

I was so hungry for your love. I didn't know what it was. When I was four, I clearly remember you being in my room, I recall how you told me to turn on my stomach and how you rubbed Vaseline all over my anus and vagina. I heard you tell me: "There, there, kitten, it won't hurt anymore." Dad, why wouldn't it hurt anymore? What else did you do to me? And why is it you called me "kitten"? That's what you called Mom in those rare moments you were being lovey-dovey and not totally drunk yet.

From that time on I really believed you thought I was your special girl, but then after a few days you again started to verbally abuse me. Why was I so stupid that I did not see that you didn't love me as a father should love his daughter? Probably because I never saw what a normal family was like! After that first time you touched me, you would feel my breasts, pull up my skirt and look under. When you hugged me it wasn't a father's hug at all. I became scared of you and of being alone with you. But at the same time, each time you did touch me I felt I was special.

By the time I was seven or eight, my brother Robert also started to sexually abuse me. At first he'd rush into my room to catch me nude as I got dressed. A little later he'd hide in my room before I went there to change and he'd watch me from his hide-out. I knew he was there, and it scared me, yet it made me feel like he was treating me in a special way at last. In time he'd make me undress for him. Eventually, his looking also included touching. After each incident I felt so dirty and ashamed, yet I also felt that perhaps I'd be someone's special girl at last.

When I turned seventeen, I was asked to marry and I figured that at last I was special to someone. He not only touched me but he had intercourse with me. The first time never hurt at all and he never believed I was a virgin ... Was I? I'm not sure. But I felt that because I had sex I was finally going to be someone's special girl.

Dad, you tried so hard to talk me out of my marriage. When I was in my gown and veil you begged me not to go through with it. You even offered me money! I made my decision when you put your arms around me and reached around to feel my breast. I knew then that I'd never be your special girl nor would you ever love me the way a father is to love his daughter.

When you died I felt relief that at last you couldn't hurt me anymore. Yet in my mind I never accepted the reality of your death. I still somehow feel your presence and still think I'll see you whenever I see Mom.

Next month there's a family reunion for Mom. She doesn't have much longer to live. As it gets closer to our trip home, I'm so afraid. You see, the day I did get married I wiped my past from my mind. As far as I was concerned, nothing had happened that I wanted to remember. It was so easy for me to pretend I was doing great. People saw me as a confident, funny, likeable person.

What they didn't know was that, inside, I was so insecure and hungry for love. I'd been sexually harassed by teachers, brothers-in-law, superiors at work and even by my husband's friends. I never said no to their advances because I felt like the little girl of many years ago and wanted to be someone special. What a fool I was, but I never knew it!

My past abuse (sexual, verbal, emotional and physical—the beatings) has caught up to me now. I can no longer deny the damage it has left me to deal with. So, I am working very hard in therapy to rebuild my life. I still hate you, Robert, and all the men who took advantage of my desire to please in exchange for love. They took advantage of me, and they took my dignity. Love I never got, except from my husband.

I have to learn to accept that my husband's love for me is unconditional. The most important thing and the hardest thing to do now is to love myself and forgive myself for my past. I'm told I'm not responsible for what you and others did to me ... now I have to convince myself of that.

"

◆

Jeannine is thirty-five years old and has been married to "the same wonderful man" for eighteen years. They have two children, ten and fifteen. "As a child I lived in a house where you did as you were told and were never entitled to express your feelings," she says. "My father was an alcoholic and all ten of us kids lived in constant fear. By day he was a teacher. At night he escaped into a booze-induced world and became a monster."

you mean it's not normal

Julie

"
God ... you mean it's not normal:

— to be ashamed that you're a girl
— to be embarrassed to talk about your body
— to laugh when you really want to cry
— to love someone but never tell them that
— to have sex when you absolutely don't want to
— to bite your fingernails till they bleed
— to never feel you can look people "in the eye"
— to never show people something is upsetting you
— to wish you were dead
— to hold your breath and "drift away" if ever you feel you may be getting emotional
— to have a "relaxing" bath which takes a grand total of 6 1/2 minutes
— to drive across the city to purchase "women's" things
— to always be fully dressed—unless you're in the shower
— to sit up half the night ... till you're certain your husband is asleep

I am sober today, and terrified! The fog has lifted and it hurts to see what is left behind. I am a terrified, angry, guilt-ridden and lonely person even though I am surrounded by friends. I am feeling emotions that are foreign to me and I don't have my "medicine" to once again numb all of these feelings. I never had the courage to deal with the abuse or any of the other emotional scars I acquired during my life. If ever there was a time when feelings would try to surface I would simply push them back down with booze.

Now, although I know alcohol is not the answer, I still have days where I would rather take the easier, softer way—DRINK. I do know, however, that drinking will only weaken the pain for that moment and when the effects of the alcohol are gone, I am then left with the original pain plus the added feelings of guilt and remorse. I have had a taste of what life can be, yet my fears and lingering self-hate make the journey so painful and seemingly worthless. I want to quit or get out, but they tell me the only way out is "through!"

It's as if I am surrounded by a ring of fire and the way to reach freedom is by going through the flames to get to the outside. I'm terrified, standing in the centre of this burning hell, and I try to walk through. The flames begin to cause pain and I take one more step. I feel the vast openness and freedom on the other side, but it is so foreign to me that I turn and run back through the flames. It is not a joyful experience to remain in the heat of the surrounding inferno but it is here that I am most comfortable, so I again choose to stay. Many times I have burned myself, but deep down my fears of the unknown overshadow the myths that on the other side is freedom and a beautiful way to live. I seem to be most comfortable being uncomfortable.

It's pretty earth-shattering to realize that the answer must come from within when you are certain your within is totally empty. You're a vacuum waiting for a force from the outside to collapse walls which have no inner supports.

I have to somehow build these necessary supports if I ever want to survive with any kind of peace and serenity. They tell me it will be hard—but it can be done. I now pray that they are right.

hope

I've thrown away the bottle. For the first time, I am out in this world, on my own.

My alcohol dependency is a crutch—a tool with which I fashioned some kind of survival. It's ironic—discarding "my medicine" is my first step in finally feeling alive.

Now I see that for many years, my emotions have not grown. I used to think I was never really a child. That I was always an adult, running wild. But now that the child in me has come out I see the truth. My emotional growth stopped on that black day so long ago. I thought I had survived— and I had. But I didn't even begin to mend.

I've always been scared of the unknown, dreading the idea of anything new. But now I see that what I've been most afraid of is me. From an early age I always had to cover my tracks, and this running created inner rage. The running and the rage made me forget the important things, the things that come from the heart. Hope—I knew what that small word meant and I prayed for it at the moment when I was first used as an object of abuse and sexuality, as a little girl, so long ago. But my prayers were not answered and that bleak day ended with a little mind full of questions and no words with which to ask questions.

Hope is "the feeling that what one desires will happen." For me it faded fast and I learned to trust no one. I couldn't accept anything. My mind tossed with: "Why? Why? Why?"

My hope became the hope that when I dulled the pain with my "medicine" it would last. I hoped for something that could never come true. I hoped to magically erase the entire memory of the past and never feel so blue again.

What I am striving for now is to work through the past openly and not allow my fears to put up a guard again. I have to somehow be honest about my true feelings. For me this is very hard. With the help of friends and counsellors I have to keep tearing down the walls—those safety walls that I used to quickly rebuild after the tiniest little fall.

I live by these two lists: my "I will nevers" and my "I wills."

I will never forget what happened to me as a small, defenceless child! I will never forget the fears and warped beliefs that made me think I had really gone wild! I will never forget the feelings of hatred that were branded in my mind during that time! I w-i-l-l n-e-v-e-r f-o-r-g-e-t any of this, but I CAN slowly deal with all the negatives of this crime!

These are my "I wills":

I will one day look into a mirror and like what's looking back. I will one day feel that I am, for once in my life, on the right track. I will one day feel that I have a right to be on this earth. I will one day feel that I have worth. I will one day truly accept what has happened to me. I will one day feel that I am finally set free.

I will one day love and be loved. For this I have HOPE.

"

♦

Julie is forty-nine years old. The daughter of devoted French Catholics, she was the fifth child in a family of eight. She is married and had four children. "My childhood memories are skimpy," she says. "My flashbacks started when I was visiting my sister. Her year-old grandchild was visiting and I wouldn't let anyone take her anywhere unless I was there. It was very important to me that she be protected at all times. I realized I was reliving my past ... I was severely burned by my father. He came after me with an iron when I was trying to get away from him because he was doing bad things to me. I was two and my older sister saw him do it. He made her tell everyone that she did it. I was gang-raped by my father and two other men when I was five or six. At seven or eight years of age, I was made to please the parish priest. From the time I was eight until I was twelve, my father abused me ... My father died when I was twelve, from an accident at work. I remember going to see him in the hospital. He gave me a look which said, "Don't tell!" I didn't understand the look then, but I sure do now ... All my family has been very supportive during this turn of events. I have been in a survivor's group but I am not in any group right now. I am trying to deal with the memories on my own. Writing this has been beneficial to me. It has helped me vent some of my anger, frustration and confusion ... I am a grandmother now—with four grandchildren. They are all a delight!"

shame

E.J.

Shame
   I finally beat you;
for once
   you didn't win out.
It was only a small battle
   a small victory
But—it was my victory
   not yours.
Your death-like grip over me
   Strangling my very soul
      has weakened.
You've lost some of your power
   I will be victorious again
You are weakening
   I am becoming stronger
I have tasted the reward.

Deep, dark, painful secrets
   Brought out into the light
Held gently and respectfully
   by another
Eye contact
   all the difference in the world
Reflecting back
   care and acceptance.

Yes Shame—
   you are weakening
Your power cannot match
   the power of a loving, caring look.

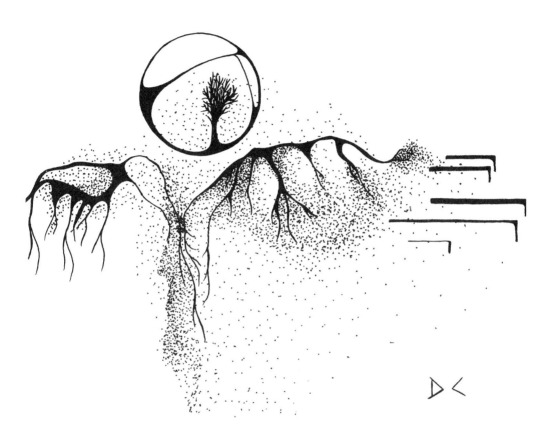

reaching out:

the struggle to be whole

interview with Sue Evans

Part Four

Q. Can you talk a little bit about the A.A. model and how you perceived its impact on women?

A. I think the A.A. model has saved millions and millions of lives. I have nothing but admiration for the program as a whole. But I think women have had to work to find a fit for themselves. The A.A. model is based on the old-style male alcoholic who was pretty rigid and grandiose and defended.

Q. Defended?

A. Defended. Protected by psychological barriers like: "I'm going to do what I am going to do and nobody is going to stop me. And my life is fine and I'm fine." The A.A. model is based on breaking through those defenses. It is based on letting his humanity come out, letting his power-lessness come out, because he has had such control in his life and his work. And that was his job—to be in control.

   Women on the other hand, in general, do not need any help in get-ting in touch with their powerlessness. So that model of trying to break through the defenses doesn't work for women because they are coming from a very different psychological standpoint. Certainly women get "defended" as their addiction grows, so the model is not totally off for women. I think there are more similarities than differences among alco-holic men and women. But I think there are differences in how women go about getting help. I think they need to get in touch with their power, rather than their powerlessness. Women need to feel the strength and the connection with people.

Q. Have you seen women struggling with A.A. and not being able to make use of it effectively?

A. Yes. Absolutely. The hardest struggle that I have seen is with the belief in God. The Christian approach in A.A. doesn't work for people of other faith backgrounds. There is a need for a broader spiritual base than that. Often, for women, their use of alcohol and drugs does not fit in with their religious beliefs and they feel cut off from their spiritual beliefs.

The A.A. model was designed for men, and women need to translate the information into words that fit for them. The reference to a male God is not appropriate for many women, especially those who have been abused by their fathers and/or father figures.

People coming into the program are very vulnerable, they are very needy. There was some "thirteen-stepping" going on—where older male sponsors were being sexual with young, newly-recovering women who didn't have the boundaries, didn't know how to protect themselves. I think there were women being victimized in that system. I don't think it is the A.A. system that did it. I think that happens in society at all levels.

I refer a lot of women to Women for Sobriety. It is much more pro-women, much more focused on women claiming their power. I always suggest several options. But addicted women do need something outside of therapy. Therapy is not enough.

Q. Can you talk briefly about what a relationship with a therapist can do for a person? And also talk about therapists knowing their boundaries?

A. I think people have healed in many different ways. My bias, of course, is that having a knowledgable therapist to help you walk through the process makes it immeasurably easier. But even under the best circumstances it's excruciating. I really am amazed at people healing themselves without the help of a knowledgable person. The therapeutic process, to me, is just having someone who stays a step ahead of you, who knows the process, who knows some exercises to help you do your work. It's not any magic, it's having a safe relationship with somebody, where you feel solid enough in the trust that you can do the hard work. You've to do it by yourself, you've got to face the feelings—but sometimes the only thing that keeps you going is that bond with the therapist, who can prod you along a little and say, "Come on, come on, come on, let's go. I'm here, I'm listening, I'm with you! You are not alone."

At certain points in the healing process, the therapeutic relationship works best in a group setting. I think relationships are what heal the damage from abuse. You don't heal from a therapist or anyone else telling you the right technique, or the right this or that. You heal by placing yourself in the hands of other people whom you can trust, who listen to you—and you let them care. That's why I think groups are better than individual work, that's why my bias is to put people in groups. Because people can always say, "Oh well, Sue's trained for it," or "She's heard everything," or "I pay her to be nice to me." Whereas in a group, with peers, you can hear, "I felt the same thing, I know what you are going through, hey I don't think you are bad." You let it in on a very different level.

Still, some women find groups to be overwhelming. And, at some points in the process, individual counselling is more healing than groups—and at other points self-help and 12 step work is best.

Q. What about therapists knowing boundaries?

A. That is a whole major issue because it's such a delicate relationship in the healing process that you have to be really respectful. You have to be really cognizant of the recovering person's boundaries because you have so much power in the relationship. A therapist, even a feminist therapist, has more power than the client just by her role, just by having more information on the client than the client has on you as a clinician. And when somebody is in trouble and comes to you and assumes because you are in a professional role that you know what is best for her, and she pays you money—all of that says that you have great potential for healing. There is also great potential for harm in all that. If the therapist has been violated herself, if the therapist has unclear boundaries, if the therapist has needs that aren't being met outside, say she is going through a divorce and is particularly needy—it's too easy to get needs met through a client in that kind of relationship. There is a lot of power for the therapist, in the beginning of therapy in particular, and you are up on a pedestal. People say, "You are saving my life!" It's really easy to be seduced by that.

Sometimes, later on, there is transference, where the client says, "You are the worst of them all." I hate to be up on that pedestal because you know you are going to come tumbling down. Boundaries have to be respected. You have to ask questions such as "Whose needs are being met?" My job as a clinician is: to take care of myself in all the ways I need to, so that my needs aren't going to slip out and wash all over the client; and to address the therapeutic needs of the client. If I am not clear about that, or if I am under stress or particularly vulnerable, I pull back, I work less, I try to find other ways of working. Because a person coming to therapy is totally vulnerable. We all know that it is not right for therapists to be sexual with their clients, but you can violate boundaries even by asking, "Do me a favour and run down to the store for me, I need some milk or something." Then you are recreating the abuse in the family, you are recreating the role imbalance between the parents and the kid. You are saying to the client, "You be the one in charge." Or, "I'm needing you." This is just an extension of the abuse.

Q. So, in a good therapist-client relationship the client will learn boundaries from the therapist.

A. Absolutely. My job is to hold my own boundaries so that I can be a model for what appropriate boundaries are. It holds clients to their boundaries—maybe they didn't have boundaries taught to them properly in their own families, so they never had an arena in which to learn.

If you don't know about appropriate boundaries, you can't know about accountability, and you don't know how to take care of yourself. You can't know how to: keep dangerous situations out; and also how to open up to let people become close to you. People with boundary problems get into a rigid stance where they either let everything in or keep everything out.

The problem with this, of course, is that we need different stances at different times. When we are on the street we need lots of boundaries. When we are being intimate or sexual in a loving, caring relationship, we need to drop our boundaries and be able to merge. It is a dance of coming together and moving apart with the people in our lives, and knowing how to do that. People who have had boundary violations don't get that knowledge.

So, in appropriate parenting or appropriate therapeutic relationships, there are certain behaviours that I need to attend to. If I become too intrusive or start needing or hit a client or become sexual with her—it's an intrusive, abusive way of hurting that client.

On the other hand, if I neglect her and don't do certain things that I need to do, I am just as damaging. It's harder to see sometimes—what could or should have happened, but didn't. For instance, if a client tries to ask intrusive questions of me or is not respectful of my professional boundaries, then I need to become really rigid and make my professional boundaries very clear so that they get the lesson, they get the reaction, so that they know they were out of line. It's very shame-provoking and it's really hard to do, but it is some of the best learning they can get. It's a reality check.

Q. So that's where appropriate shame comes in?

A. Yes. Absolutely. Shame is a learning tool and if you don't have shame—you've got baby psychopaths walking around. Shame is what socializes us. It teaches us appropriate and inappropriate behaviour. But when it becomes connected to the identity, it becomes dangerous and harmful to the person.

Q. What about grieving. Grieving the lost time, the lost childhood, the lost nurturing back then, the lost opportunities, the loss of all that comes with a happy childhood? Is that important?

A. Very much so. I think grieving is a big part of healing. Not just for what you suffered but what didn't happen. Relationships, love, innocence, accountability—all the things you never had and never will have in that context. At the beginning of healing, people grieve for what happened—the abuse that they suffered. Later, they grieve at a deeper level for more subtle things—what didn't happen. But it's like a corkscrew, the victimized person grieves over the same issues again and again, but at a deeper level as they heal. It's very important and it's very hard.

Q. Sue, what are the implications of the systemic point of view—seeing your own abuse as part of a system of abuse? Why is it difficult, and how is it healing?

A. I think in part it is difficult because abuse is such a personal thing. It is hard to step back and see the larger picture when you are the one that it was done to, or when it is being done to you now. It feels so focused and targeted on you.

Understanding from the systemic point of view doesn't mean that the abuser isn't accountable. It doesn't let him (or her) off the hook. And it doesn't mean you don't have to feel the feelings of the abuse, because in order to heal, you do. You've still got to do the emotional work.

It's like the difference between looking at one alcoholic family and looking at the larger culture. There is relief for women to see that we share some similarities, we share some of the same struggles, we share some of the same processes of surviving in this culture. It gives us a sense of, "Hey, I'm not crazy. It's not just me. There is a bigger picture happening here and I'm responding to certain stresses that are common to women."

There is the same kind of relief when you can look at the larger family as a whole system. You realize, "Hey. It's not that Dad hated me the most. It's like he had all that stress. He and mom were wierd, they didn't like each other. He had a favourite sister over here, etc." You are able to depersonalize the situation. You are able to see bigger than yourself, bigger than your own particular pain.

Q. I think that many people would feel minimized by that. Can you address that feeling? What you would do with it?

A. Well that's interesting. I think that is related to being a shame-based person—whatever happens, your focus is on how bad you are. There is a lot of narcissism in shame. It's like, "Oh my God, the whole world is looking at me, everybody thinks I'm stupid, oh why did I ever … " And then you have that sense that, "It's me and it's directed to me, and I'm the worst of them all and he hates me the most, etc." It is a developmental stage that people are stuck at. You know, we all go through it. When we are little kids the sun rises and sets on us and that's important. And it's important that kids get full attention, total love etc. so that they can grow and develop into empathetic people. You fill up enough, and then you get to notice other people and their needs. I think shame-based people never get full, they never get that total adoration and attention. And so they are stuck at that same narcissistic level.

Kids say, "Aren't I wonderful." Shame-based people say, "I'm the worst of the worst." It's still narcissistic, it's just negative. And to feel diminished by seeing yourself as "just" part of that system is part of that shame.

To see the big picture is to say, "I'm not the centre of how bad every-thing is, and what caused all the awfulness." It is spreading the account-ability.

Q. Can you walk the reader through that a bit. How do you step into think-ing systemically if you have a shame-based identity and are a shame-based thinker?

A. I think doing a genogram is very powerful. Where you write out family relationships for several generations back and identify who in the fam-ily had chemical problems, who had emotional abuse, who had emo-tional difficulties, etc. You lay it out and you go back as many generations as you can and it becomes very clear that chemical depend-ency and abuse are systemic. It is not just something that happened to you, it is part of the entire family system, and in most cases if you don't know about it, it's only because you are not in on the secret.

Q. When a person sees that, when a person understands that this is part of her whole family and she somehow shifts the focus from herself and get over feeling diminished, what happens?

A. I think there is a major relief in saying "Hey, I'm not the sick one, or the biggest victim or the bad one." But there is an element of grief, over the realisation that it's not even personal enough. Take the example of kids running around getting in trouble. They want attention, so they run around and break stuff and knock lamps over until they get smacked. They would rather get smacked than be ignored. If you are getting any kind of attention, it's better than being invisible. And when you are dealing with this systemic understanding, you realize, "Hey, it's not even personal. We're so disengaged that it wasn't even about me." That in itself causes grief. So there is a sense of relief but there is also empti-ness.

When people have trouble letting go of the shame, saying, "I'm the victim, I'm the wrong one, everything I do is wrong, etc.," I think it's be-cause the shame is functional. I think it is working to protect them. One thing it does is give them some sense of control or impact, which is preferable to feeling the total helplessness of being a victim. So if you are hanging onto the shame it's because it's better than feeling so little, so helpless, and hopeless with nowhere to turn. I mean, that's excrucia-ting for people and they will often do anything to prevent how "little" that makes them feel.

Q. And if you can face up to that?

A. Feel the feelings and it all kind of shifts and settles into the realisation that, "Yeah, everybody's got a part and what was, was." And you ask, how can you live your life now so that it doesn't happen again? How can you take charge, how can you take your life back again?

Q. So again, you say, feel those feelings and then something else can happen instead?

A. I think that we do lots of twisting to try to *not* feel the feelings and its an amazing thing that people live through any of this, it's like a testimony to the survival of the human spirit. I don't really understand why it is that some people can live through torture, through incredible experiences, and come through stronger.

I think there is nobody more damaged than an untreated victim but I think there is nothing stronger than those who have done the work, have done the therapy, have come through it. They have depth in themselves, they can live through anything. They have been handed the worst and they have come through it—so what else is there?

If you can get through it, it is like the sword being tempered by fire; if you can get through it, you are stronger for it. There may, of course, in your inner, inner, inner workings still be a shame-base and a kind of uncertain identity, and you may be acting like a real adult while inside feeling really little sometimes, but I think survivors are miracles.

In general, I think its true for a lot of recovering people—they are brilliant people, kind, sensitive, incredibly intuitive, really, really incredible people in totally unmanageable situations. And they needed to do whatever they needed to do to survive, whether that was drink, go into trance and dissociate, whatever—in part because of how wonderful they were. And if they can reclaim that, if they can get back to themselves, nothing is going to stop them. So much good has come from people being able to heal themselves and take charge of their lives.

ways of seeing

perspectives on survivors and substance abuse

Barbara Ball

I write this article as a helper, and, of course, all my life experience informs me and shapes me, and both helps and hinders me in carrying out that role of helper. That is especially true of those experiences, which we've all had, of feeling vulnerable, powerless and ashamed.

In a marginal or technical way, I could say I speak as a survivor. As a young child, I ran home several times to disclose incidents of sexual abuse, ranging from the old man on the railway bridge at Lindsey Street, to the young man on the monkey bars at City Park, and including the mother of my best friend (when I was seven).

These experiences were definitely frightening, even terrifying. I felt guilty. I was not supposed to go on monkey bars, but fortunately my parent listened, comforted me and told me it wasn't my fault at all (even for going on the monkey bars). My feelings were validated, the police were called and the messages I got were that the men (who were never caught) had done something criminal. These experiences are not comparable to incest.

Because I could do what I needed to do at the time, I worked through the feelings. I don't feel the "survivor" identity as strongly for those experiences as I do for for other experiences in my life, such as having cancer, and being a hospital patient.

I haven't had the personal experience of substance abuse either, although I've been close to people and families who have. These experiences of alcoholism are what led me to have an interest in addiction, and to work and study in the area of addiction and families.

I've worked for the last six years at the Women's Post Treatment Centre. Our client group is made up of women who have had problems with chemical dependency, and histories of childhood sexual abuse. Our program is based on the assumption that, for many women, adult chemical abuse problems are related to earlier sexual abuse. "Post Treatment" refers to post "addiction" treatment.

140

If I needed another title for this article, it might be "The Tyranny of the One Right Perspective," and I want to focus on why I think it is so important to have several ways of understanding substance abuse and addiction, and also several perspectives on the *functions* of substance abuse.

Prior to 1983, when I had studied substance abuse and addiction, nearly all of the available literature was based on the notion of "disease." All substance abuse problems were seen as being basically the same—involving predictable phases, stages and symptoms. I can recall a phrase in one book: "all alcoholics are as alike as peas in a pod."

I was steeped in the medical model, and the beliefs about alcoholism and drug addiction that stem from this viewpoint. And I could see the value of this understanding. It was useful for removing guilt, shame, self blame: "I drank because I had a disease ... It wasn't my fault." Alcoholics Anonymous is based on the disease model and on the notion of insanity. And that program works well for many people.

I could also see the value for helpers, in the medical model. There was value in becoming very knowledgeable about the phases, stages, signs and symptoms of substance abuse. Otherwise, certain problems would remain unrecognized, when often they were the primary problems. Denial is certainly very real, and helpers can collude in denial.

But I could also see problems with this viewpoint. Virtually everyone I worked with who had developed chronic chemical abuse patterns, had experienced so much pain and trauma in their life that I could see chemical dependency was a way that they had coped and survived. I wasn't the only one who could see this either. A lot of the people with whom I worked had trouble accepting or understanding chemical abuse as a disease. I recall several people saying "If it hadn't been for drugs or alcohol I'd be dead," or, "I'd be insane." I believed them then, and I still believe today that their assessments were correct.

A second and more serious problem was that I began to see the idea of disease as one that masked or hid other problems. I was very concerned about the fact that if we see substance abuse *only* as a disease, we don't have to look at the reality of the sexual abuse, and the function of the sexual abuse—which is to numb the pain. The "disease" concept assists us to deny the reality of sexual abuse.

This denial reflects the denial in our society. And denial of sexual abuse is still a huge issue. Substance abuse must be seen as a survival strategy, and understood from that perspective—especially when it is related to the traumatic effects of childhood sexual abuse. Substance abuse can be viewed as an indicator of earlier abuse and, certainly, as a same and rational act.

I believe we need all of these perspectives, and others, and that we need to be able to see two separate problems: substance abuse and childhood sexual abuse. Of course, if we see substance abuse problems *only* as symptoms of earlier sexual abuse, we can fall into the error of assuming that substance abuse is going to simply disappear when the underlying sexual abuse issues are dealt with. This is certainly not always the case.

The way we understand problems determines the kinds of solutions we develop. If we see all substance abuse problems as part of one disease, we are going to be caught in the "tyranny of the one right way." I think (to focus on treatment for a moment) we need to understand and assess, with the individual, "the job" that the drug or alcohol is doing for them.

That brings me to my second point. Certainly, substance abuse is about numbing the pain, but it is about other things too.

Most of our pain involves being hurt by people close to us. We feel violated, betrayed, hurt by people, and then we are not able to trust. And when you can't trust, substances function as an alternative to people. Moreover, I believe that substance abuse is an attempt to find a feeling of closeness or intimacy, when the isolation becomes too overwhelming.

It is also an attempt to become someone else, when you are filled with self-hatred and self-loathing. Thus, substance abuse functions as a defence against pain, memory, feelings, history.

I think it is important to broaden and deepen our understanding of complex social problems like substance abuse, and I encourage reading and exploring the views offered by others. For example, Marion Woodman offers a thought provoking perspective on substance abuse. In her view, addiction is more than numbing the pain. It is a search for meaning in life and food for a hungry soul. She refers to addiction as the inner energy that drives an individual towards a particular object—whether that object is food, drugs, alcohol or another person. She portrays this addiction as a drive towards a substitute for something that remains unknown, a drive which comes from a sense of absence, an emptiness. Addiction is based on longing for presence, not just an escape from something intolerable. It is a search for perfection.

She goes on to say that, in our society, perfection is confused with reality. Unless you pretend to be perfect you don't belong—you are considered weird, neurotic, unfit. She gives us the example of the dysfunctional family pretending to be happy. In this example, denial is fundamental—denial of what is *not* present, a loving family. Think about how reality has been shattered for the abused child: addicted persons have experienced trauma and can't trust reality. We all need to be able to rely on our own perception of what is real, but abused children have had the ground pulled out from under them. There is an absence of trust at the core of their being.

In Woodman's view, instead of looking outside of ourselves and trying to transcend ourselves, we need to move into ourselves. She says we need to talk about "human unsuccess." This does not mean failure, but the "unsuccess" that is human, in contrast to perfection that "rapes the soul." She also mentions the "wisdom" in addiction which leads a person to ask, "Who am I? What is this compulsion?" As Woodman says, "if we become stuck in a way of life that is not right for us or a psychological attitude that we've outgrown, then symptoms appear that force us out of the nest." The craving for alcohol represents the spiritual thirst of our quest for wholeness.

In conclusion I want to emphasize that social problems like child abuse and substance abuse are complex. We need to keep looking for alternative ways of viewing and understanding them. Our bias gets in the way of our ability to see other views—our bias determines what we emphasize. I am aware that my training has influenced me to look at our society, and also to look at psychology and spirituality, for my understanding. I've tended to de-emphasize the physical. I was really struck by that recently, when I saw a TV program demonstrating the work being done with infants who are born addicted to crack. This program made me very aware of my bias, because it sharply emphasized the physical. I watched the images of these tiny bodies, wracked and writhing with physical pain in every nerve ending. It seems important to remind ourselves of the physical reality of addiction. For those babies addiction is not about numbing the pain—*addiction is the pain.*

the twelve steps modified

Sherry

"

For a long time, women, particularly survivors of childhood sexual abuse and other forms of abuse, have had a tough time with the language of the Twelve Steps. The language is often perceived as moralistic, formal and archaic. There is an underlying expectation that women should "let go" of the past and forgive those who have hurt them. This is often inappropriate for women who are in the process of healing from the past, and is the difficulty women in general, and survivors in particular, have with the Twelve Steps. From my own experience and the experience of others, I recognize that the Twelve Steps are a useful tool for growth. However, I believe that it is time to make the Steps more accessible by modifying the language.

This particular feminist version of the Twelve Steps was birthed at the "Beyond Survival: Women, Identity, and Addiction" conference in Toronto (April, 1989). A group of women came together in a one-day workshop facilitated by the staff of the Women's Post Treatment Centre to discuss addictions and childhood abuse. The major focus of the workshop was the difficulty women in general, and survivors in particular, have with the Twelve Steps. In response to this discussion, I submitted a rough draft of the modified Twelve Steps.

The intention of this modified version is to prompt further discussion. This version of the Twelve Steps is not endorsed by any of the Twelve Step programs, but it does provide another perspective on recovery. I invite you to take what fits, to discuss alternatives, and to discover a version with which you are comfortable.

disease model: twelve steps

1. We admitted that we were powerless over _____, that our lives had become unmanageable.
2. We came to believe that a power greater than ourselves could restore us to sanity.
3. We made a decision to turn our will and our lives over to the care of God as we understood Him.
4. We made a fearless and searching moral inventory of ourselves.
5. We admitted to God, to ourselves, and to another human being the exact nature of our wrongs.
6. We were entirely ready to have God remove all these defects of character.
7. We humbly asked Him to remove our shortcomings.
8. We made a list of all persons we had harmed, and became willing to make amends to them all.
9. We made direct amends to such people wherever possible, except when to do so would injure them or others.
10. We continued to take personal inventory and when we were wrong promptly admitted it.
11. We sought through prayer and meditation to improve our conscious contact with God as we understood Him, praying only for knowledge of His will for us and the power to carry that out.

12. Having had a spiritual awakening as a result of these steps, we tried to carry this message to _____, and to practice these principles in all our affairs.

feminist model: twelve steps

1. Admitted we have a problem and recognized that our social environment contributes to our problem.
2. Recognized that help is available and that there are other ways of coping.
3. Became willing to change and asked for help.
4. Looked at both our healthy and unhealthy behaviours and coping skills.
5. Broke the silence—shared our lives, our pain, and our joy with others.
6. Became teachable; became willing to learn new healthy behaviours to replace our unhealthy behaviours.
7. Began to forgive ourselves and others.

8. Accepted responsibility for the harm we caused ourselves and others, recognizing that we do not need to take responsibility for those who harmed us.
9. Did what we could, without harming ourselves or others, to repair these damages and not repeat the unhealthy behaviour.
10. Took responsibility for our day to day behaviour, recognizing both our healthy and unhealthy behaviours.
11. Developed our individual spirituality, seeking inner wisdom and strength.
12. As a result of on-going healing and growth, we tried to live happier, healthier lives; learning to love and accept ourselves as we are.

May your journeys bring great joy and awareness.

"

◆

"I am a recovering addict who is currently employed by the Elizabeth Fry Society as coordinator of Women's Choices: A Drug and Alcohol Awareness Program. *My recovery has involved an ongoing struggle, on both the personal and professional level, with traditional methods of understanding addiction. The journey through recovery has led me to a feminist/social model which recognizes the broad range of coping skills that women use to survive in a sexist society."*

A.A. and unfinished business

Esther S.

"

I am a thirty-eight-year-old single parent. I am also a recovered alcoholic. I have been a member of Alcoholics Anonymous for almost thirteen years. Soon I will have had eight years of continuous sobriety.

I have been seeing a counsellor at the Women's Post Treatment Centre for fifteen-and-a-half months. This has saved my life—it has given me life. For the first time I know that I am free, I know I'm okay. For the first time I have an understanding of what I feel, and why. More important, I realize my feelings are not "wrong." I was abused as a child. I come from a dysfunctional home. These things shaped my feelings and led me into relationships that could not work and that were abusive. I couldn't understand why I was so depressed, my first two years in A.A. I worked hard at the program and I had a God and I was very involved in A.A. I went for out-patient counselling and I had an excellent counsellor and I learned a lot about myself and about alcoholism.

I did a very thorough Step 4 and I had a wonderful person with whom I did my Step 5. I wanted to do Steps 8 and 9, but couldn't. Every time I thought about it or talked about it, the resentment and hurt were overwhelming. I couldn't understand why this was so. I believed what I was taught in A.A., that I was to concern myself with what I had done and not what had been done to me. Any time I talked about my feelings, I was told by people in A.A. that I had self-pity, that I had no acceptance, that my Step 3 was no good, that I had taken my "will" back, that I needed to do another Step 4. No matter what I tried, nothing worked. No one told me that I had been abused and needed help.

I got drunk after two years of sobriety.

I knew drinking was not the answer. After nine days I went into treatment. I learned more about myself, the A.A. program and alcoholism. I did another Step 3, 4 and 5. And this time I did Steps 8 and 9.

A year later I drank again and again sobered up almost immediately. One-and-a-half years later I drank again for four days and sobered up one last time. Five-and-a-half years after that, I sought professional help and learned that I came from a dysfunctional home, that I had been very badly abused as a child and that I had a lot of unfinished business to take care of. At that time, I had been in A.A. for almost ten years and had had almost five years of sobriety. I was dying inside. The hurt, the pain, the rage and the anxiety were almost unbearable. I could not understand what was happening to me. I thought I was going insane in spite of being sober. I thought I was doing something wrong in spite of the fact that I had what was considered "good" sobriety. I was terrified and very confused and disillusioned. It was like living in hell on earth.

My doctor suggested that I go to the Women's Post Treatment Centre, so I contacted them and put my name on the waiting list. I was very fortunate, for at that time there was a wait of only five months.

There, I learned that what I was experiencing wasn't self-pity; it was reality. I had been abused and I was in a lot of pain and I was very angry and it was "okay" to feel those things. I learned to accept that I had been abused. I already knew from A.A. not to blame and not to use what had been done to me as an excuse for my inadequacies today.

For the first time in my life, I could understand why I felt what I was feeling—and that it had nothing to do with alcoholism or doing the steps incorrectly, or me being crazy. For the first time, I felt safe enough to talk about my feelings and know that I was being totally accepted. I wasn't being looked down upon, or ostracized because I still felt so much anger and hurt and rage and resentment and bitterness, bewilderment and fear, after all my years in A.A. For the first time I could heal, and cry for the child who was never allowed to be. For the first time in my life I have self-esteem and it's not contingent upon how my day was, or who and what is around me. I needed to get to the root of my problems—I needed abuse counselling.

Since going to the Women's Post Treatment Centre I have run into several women in A.A. who have gone for abuse counselling at the same place as I am. Our experiences are pretty much the same. We have all been told by our sponsors or other people in A.A. that we are feeling "self-pity" or we need to do another Step 4 or Step 5, or that our lack of God is our problem. We have all been told to leave the past alone, that what was done to us is in the past. "It's life," we've been told, "Let it go." We've all been fortunate enough to have reached the Women's Post Treatment Centre and the result for all of us is the same. We understand ourselves: our feelings, and why we did and do the things we do. We understand our reactions in intimate relationships, our own abuse towards our children and our fear of trusting. Today we all have more than sobriety—today we are whole, viable human beings. More and more of us survivors of child abuse are opening up at A.A. meetings and speaking about the issues that result from abuse. More and more, we are approached by women who can relate to what we are saying. They too have been abused and, yes, A.A. has arrested their alcoholism, but it is not enough. They too need the professional help that we received. The waiting list at the Women's Post Treatment Centre has over one hundred names, I am told, and the wait is longer than a year. That is too long when one is sober and in so much pain.

And where do the men go for help? Many men in A.A. have been abused. There is a clinic that deals with men's abuse issues, and one man that I know was told that he would have to wait for a year, and not to bother putting his name on the waiting list. It sounded like he needed help immediately—where does he go?

Our children are our most precious commodity. We adults who have been abused as children cannot expect to bring up our children in a healthy fashion. We need help. We need more places like the Women's Post Treatment Centre. We need more counsellors who specialize in abuse issues. We have the chance today to break the cycle of dysfunctinal families and raise our children in healthy, non-abusive homes. I don't want my daughter to have to seek professional help when she is thirty because of what was done to me.

Every time my daughter acts in an inappropriate way for any length of time, I question, "Is this a stage she is going through? Is this 'normal' or is this because of me and my past?" That is my reminder today of my past. If I accomplish nothing else in my life, I want to raise my daughter in a healthy environment. I believe today that this is possible and that it is already happening.

"

♦

Esther S. lives with her school-aged daughter, works part-time in a creative profession, and attends university.

"It has been four years since a professional told me that I had been abused," she says. "I didn't know what 'healthy' or 'normal' was. Just a short while ago, after I had finished counselling at the WPTC, my memory of being raped by a stranger at the age of seven returned. It was frightening—I thought I was losing my mind—and very painful. I had suppressed it for thirty-three years. But it answered my question about what made me the way I am ... I could never figure out why I could only go so far in A.A. and then there would be another crisis. I was totally driven, especially in relationships ... I was adopted and I never really felt I belonged. My family was very dysfunctional, and my parents were not emotionally healthy, although they were not alcoholic ... I have wanted to go to university for twenty years, but I never had the confidence to do it. It was only because of the counselling process that I was able to finally do it. I look at the process like this: A.A. got me into abuse counselling, and abuse counselling has allowed me to make sense of things and integrate my experience ... In a way it's harder now. I have a real responsibility to myself and my daughter. There are no more excuses. Counselling was very hard too. But the results have been worth it."

there was something wrong and it didn't have anything to do with working my program incorrectly

Ruby Tuesday

"

Since the age of twelve, I have been given a variety of labels by mental health professionals. I have been labelled a manic depressive, a schizophrenic, an alcoholic. The last psychiatrist I saw went easy on me, God bless him. He just said I was a little neurotic. There was hope after all!

I spent quite a few years in A.A. but found this was not the answer for me. I found many of the clichés, repeated to me almost robotically, to be defeating in my quest for healing. Clichés such as: "live and let live," "forgive and forget," "the past is the past," "today is the first day in the rest of your life"—they all reinforced the theme that I was to blame. I was constantly told to "work harder on my program." I thought there was something seriously wrong with me because I still felt so horrible. I found out later, when my memories started popping through, that there really was something wrong—but it sure didn't have anything to do with working my program incorrectly.

My memories of past sexual and physical abuse began to emerge three years ago and I have been in counselling at a women's health clinic ever since.

I have a problem with alcohol when I am involved in an intimate relationship that includes sex. I still have the tendency to get involved with unsafe men and so I drink fountains in order to feel safe. But the consequences of this behaviour are that I leave myself more unsafe because I'm either blacked out or my judgement is impaired. It seems like I don't care about what happens to me but the fact is that I am repeating a pattern from childhood. I think I am the child without any boundaries and the booze helps me to "space out." I'm working on sorting this out.

Poetry, painting, writing in my journal and seeing my counsellor are the methods I find effective for healing.

Lately I have added guitar playing—I find it soothing and also rewarding to learn a new skill. I am presently finishing one degree at university and will begin my second in the fall. If it all works out I'll soon be a teacher.

God bless my counsellor at Klinic. She has played a big part in turning my life around. She is the first person who believed me; the first person who hasn't minimized any of my experience. I can scream, rant and swear about what I've been through and how I feel. Most importantly, she told me I didn't have to forgive. What a wonderful revelation!

"

♦

Ruby Tuesday is a thirty-year-old caucasian and a single parent of two daughters, aged five and six.

transition

Ruby Tuesday

I said to self
"a new carving
of the mask
must take place"
though I knew
the carving
had begun
some months before,
in the beginnings
of my metamorphosis.
And while I struggle
to shed
those stubborn pieces
of exoskeleton
still adhered
to the core of me
the voice of
my soul
speaks:
Keep the faith,
Keep the faith,
For so to become
the butterfly
you must die a
thousand times
and only then
will you be set
free.

I am yesterday

Ruby Tuesday

I am yesterday
an eclipsed highway
a trinket spoon
a slivered moon
the fragment of a dream
a jezebel redeemed
a bluebell in the shade
that has begun to fade
into my yesterday.

keeping the spirit in my life

Louise

"
One of the things I liked about A.A. was the way it presented finding your higher power as a personal choice. But after I reached sobriety there were still things that were missing from my life. I had no real identity and almost no memory of my childhood.

I had some flashbacks and spoke to a priest about them. He knew the abuser I was referring to and he said: "It is not possible." I thought, "If it's not, I must be crazy!" I prayed that it be taken from me until I found someone to talk to about it.

I exposed myself to native ceremonies and teachings in spurts. (My whole life has been based on mistrust, so I always do things in spurts.) I found my identity when I started to live the traditional way of life, following the sweetgrass trail.

A combination of being in A.A. plus being involved in the culture prepared me to be strong during the healing process. It was like taking steps, but I didn't know that at the time. After I got sober, I found my identity— but still there was that missing part. I couldn't remember any of my childhood before I was eleven years old.

By the time I got to the Women's Post Treatment Centre I viewed my life as a jigsaw puzzle.

◆

In the culture [native Indian culture] we go by fours. By the fourth month in counselling I was ready to kill myself. I couldn't believe people could treat a little girl the way I had been treated. It was like unravelling a horror story. I was abused with dogs, with snakes, I was choked. Every four months in counselling there was a peak.

◆

I was terrified of the little girl inside me. I didn't want to look at her—I didn't want to know what she looked like.

◆

154

It just happened that I had light skin. My mom was sixteen when she had me out of wedlock, which put shame on my family. That made me different, and a target.

♦

I had a white counsellor who was great. From her I received acceptance of my abuse. She understood very little of the culture, but she was open to it.

The culture knew about sexual abuse but not the extent of it—not how awful it could be. The only way my native friends knew how to help me was by giving me spiritual and cultural support. They didn't understand the reality or long term effects of sexual abuse.

So there was very little about sexual abuse I could tell my native friends and very little about my culture I could tell my counsellor. I had to bridge the two kinds of support myself.

♦

I had been a member of A.A. for twelve years when I went to people I had known since I joined and told them my memories of sexual abuse. They didn't support me. I think it was partly because I had been sober for ten years and they thought I should have dealt with it already. Plus they didn't know how to fix it.

I didn't want them to fix it. I just wanted them to be there to listen when I needed someone. I stopped trusting anybody in A.A. because they wouldn't listen.

Now I have new A.A. friends whom I have educated. Sometimes they would say, "But I don't understand." I learned to say, "Just shut up and listen!"

♦

If I didn't have people—native friends, the people at school and the people at the WPTC—I don't think I would have made it. The culture, especially, sustained me—it provided the spiritual support I needed.

When I talk about this I want to cry. I realize how sick I was. And I can't believe I lived through it. Twice. Once living it. Once remembering it.

I think it will always hurt. It's a feeling of loss. I lost my childhood. I grew up just like that. "Snap." I lost out on receiving the basic necessities of life. I took on different personalities. I did that until I started the healing process. Shrinks would have locked me up and thrown away the key.

Now I'm learning what kids are all about, what childhood is. I've learned to be silly. I've learned how to have fun and to enjoy life.

♦

If I didn't have a spiritual way of life my healing would have taken a lot longer.

We have a body, a mind and a spirit. If we only take care of body and mind, there is no balance. There is a gap. In counselling you learn to take care of your mind—your thinking and your emotions—and, in turn, you start taking care of your body. But that is still not enough. The body and the mind only sustain us for awhile.

Having a creator—having the spirit in your life—it gives you hope. But it does more than that. It balances your mind and body. Otherwise you can spend a lot of time in counselling trying to retain what you've gained—to keep things from going out of whack again. In the counselling work I have done I have found that if people have a belief they are much easier to work with. Otherwise all you have, for lack of a better word, is technology.

♦

Some incest survivors won't agree with me on this, but I want to be free of everything to do with sexual abuse. The Creator is so kind and wants me to be free. I want to be able to forgive them all, to be free of them. I have always wanted that.

But this has not been the goal of my healing. I needed to heal emotionally and mentally and that does not entail forgiveness. I think forgiveness probably comes with how much I rely on my Creator. It sure as hell isn't going to come directly from me!

♦

I was a violent drunk because I hated myself. Through fasting, through sweats, and through dreams I grew spiritually and emotionally—and as I grew I was given more responsibilities. The messages came through me and through an elder.

I go to a female elder in the culture who gives teachings on life that are very simple—such as: women should work with women and men with men. It is not excluding one sex from the other—you have to come together to create a balance. This woman elder was also abused. She affirms that I am doing the right things. She is so loving, so kind and so humble and she has a great sense of humour. If she heard me saying these things she would say, "These things have been given to me."

♦

I was told I would work with women, especially those who were sexually abused. That was three years ago, before I had started dealing with the abuse. My reaction was, "No way!" I didn't like women and I hated men.

The way things have been happening, the people, places and things that are being put in my life are directing me to work with survivors.

♦

The majority of people in A.A., even today, do not want to hear about sexual abuse. They say, "This is not the place to deal with it." But now, if I want to deal with it in A.A., I do.

♦

Two male A.A. friends helped me a lot. One man was so upset he was hyperventilating, but he didn't stop me. He said things like, "Ooohhh ... but you were just a little girl!" That helped me see myself.

♦

The men in A.A. and in the culture have given me my idea of what brothers are. I still don't know if this is what a brother is, because I never had one. I called the uncles who abused me "my brothers" because I was brought up in their family by my maternal grandparents.

My grandmother knew these things were happening to me, maybe not how often and when, but she knew. I confronted her and she said, "No way that could have happened." But she tries in her own way to show me that she cares about me and loves me.

♦

As I went through my abuse therapy every pattern was shattered. So many personalities were destroyed. It was very frightening. I wondered, "Who the hell am I?" and "Who will I be?" I was scared and always anxious.

Every time I found a new way of dealing with things and tested it out a few times I would be thrilled. I'd feel like a little kid.

♦

I'm forty-one years old and I still wonder when I'll grow up. I have a respect for myself and dignity now that I will never let anyone take away. I have given up many people because they have chosen not to deal with me with respect and dignity.

"

♦

Louise is a single parent with two boys, aged thirteen and twenty-two. She is in her last year of a university degree in Social Work. "Things are much better now, mainly because I can talk about it (the abuse)," she says. "I feel a freedom from the abuse. But I'm still working on some long term effects of abuse.

"One of the main ones is my relationship with men. I pick scummy kinds of guys and afterwards I realize that I have been abusing myself. Then I find myself wondering, 'Why am I feeling this heaviness inside?' I realize that I'm not feeling happy and I'm getting bored.

"My form of running is not doing things I should be doing to make my day to day life easier. My running takes different forms. Like if I should be studying, I clean my house or go for coffee. It is another part of my life that I have to work on."

native spirituality

R.S.W.

"
            When I came into A.A., an elder told me
that we have to deal with each issue in our life in order to heal. One of my issues was my alcoholism, so I started dealing with that. Sexual abuse I suffered as a child and teenager was also a big issue, but first I had to deal with being an Indian.

I never denied being an Indian but I was never proud of it. I didn't understand what it meant to be an Indian—at least not the spiritual aspect.

When I was a little girl I was told I was not an Indian. My mother was an Indian and my father was part Indian—I could tell by looking at them that they were Indian—but they were ashamed of who they were. When people would ask me my nationality, I would say I'm an Indian, but I would say it in a defensive way, waiting for their reaction. I didn't know anybody who felt good about being an Indian and I was never taught anything positive about the Indian way of life. My dad would say he was Scottish and yet I could see that he was part Indian, so I was very confused and very mixed up.

So after I started dealing with my alcoholism there was a part of me that wanted to find out what it really meant to be an Indian. When I was about six months sober I started having visions when I was awake. I'd see eagles flying or a wolf just sitting there and howling or I'd see rivers or snow just falling.

When you go into A.A. you've got to find a higher power, something to depend on other than yourself to sober up, and somehow my spirit was showing me a way to go. I always believed in God but I was very confused about churches and religion because my mother was often insane when I was growing up and a lot of it was tied up with religion.

The Catholic church wouldn't baptize us because my dad didn't marry into the Catholic church and the other church wouldn't because my parents didn't go to church. When I was about ten years old my mother took us down to the river. It was very cold and there was still ice in the river. She started dunking us in this ice water. She was insane at that time.

I remember being very scared of God—her god. She would be saying, "You are going to hell if you are not baptized." It was always like God was going to punish us, like we were going to go to hell.

Another thing my mother did was make us take boxes of garbage to church to get blessed. It was around the time I was thirteen and I knew it was strange and was afraid of people thinking I was crazy. There was a lot about my mother I have to deal with as I continue to work things through.

And then there was the sexual abuse. My mother used to come after me with enemas. The last time was when I was thirteen. I was in the kitchen and I saw her coming at me with the enema. She made me lay on the couch and my sister and brothers were there and she pulled down my pants and did it. My mother had this scary, shrill laugh. I remember laying there and being really scared and hurt and humiliated, wishing she wouldn't do this to me.

I guess all through the years all this was buried inside and when I started recovering in A.A. the pain and hurt and anger would always be there. The abuse would always flash through my mind. When I would go and do my steps 4 and 5 it was always there; the pain would never go away. And it wasn't just my mother. I was abused by older boys and men when I was a little girl.

I kept away from men for a long time. I had a lot of fear of men and I also had a fear of aggressive women, which I didn't understand.

As for A.A., really deep feelings were never talked about in the club room. It was never done. It was mostly steps and some feeling stuff but nothing really deep. But A.A. helped me. I learned how to use the steps, I learned how to keep sober.

I was thirty-three when I started going to A.A. and within a year I knew I would never drink again. But it was only last year, after seven more years, that the pain inside me stopped.

So, I sobered up in 1981 after going to A.A., but I never talked about my sexual abuse and my pain from it there. I went to see an elder in 1982 and got my Indian name, and that's how I started to learn about my culture and I started my road to healing in that way. But I didn't talk about the abuse with him.

I started dealing with my sexual abuse a little later. I started by talking with the women on the reserve, sharing my sexual abuse with them. They were very shocked. But slowly, slowly they started sharing their own abuse with me. That's how it started to come out into the open.

In the beginning it was just one-to-one. We would talk for a couple of hours a day sometimes, just sharing our pain and our stories with each other. Then we started having little secret meetings. I can remember when we started having those meetings, walking down the road, being scared and thinking, "Oh, people are going to know what we're going to talk about." Then I still felt dirty, I still blamed myself. I felt ashamed. And so did the other women. They didn't want anybody to know, not their husbands, not their children, nobody. We talked in secret, and if anyone came to the door while we were having those meetings ... ! I remember jumping up and hiding in the bathroom and the other ones jumping behind the couch. It was just like we were kids and what had happened to us was so, so bad and we were so bad.

That's how we felt. It was scary to talk about something you had never talked about before. I remember having such bad headaches afterwards. And that pain, that pain, it stayed for so long.

Now I can talk about it and that pain is not there. It took eight years at least. At times I thought I was going to crack right up and I wanted to commit suicide. I just didn't want to live anymore, that pain was so bad. It was like ripping apart inside. I'd lay there at night and just shake, I would vibrate so much. And I'd hang onto my sweetgrass and my feather and I'd just shake like a leaf. And I'd be alone. My husband would sometimes say, "Oh you are crazy, you're crazy just like your mother!" he would say. Or, "You're the devil!"

Sometimes I would feel like smashing things. One time when I really started to feel my anger, I did. I smashed my coffee table and I got down on my hands and knees and was crying and crying and crying and just asking my creator, "What's wrong with me? I feel like I could kill myself or somebody else." I had never felt that kind of anger before. I was so scared of myself. That was when I was digging right in.

When I was six years sober I put myself into Pritchard House. That was when I was really shaken, I was so scared of everybody. I just kept praying. I'd use my sweetgrass and feather and I kept asking the Creator to help me. That's when I really wanted to die. But I still thought there was an end in sight. What really helped me was a poem I wrote when I was about three months sober. This is how it goes:

> "What is life?" he said to me.
> "Come and sit upon my knee.
>
> See how far the ocean spreads
> the sky in all its splendour threads.
> There is a story to unfold
>   love the peace and the
>   thunder bold
> the majestic mountains
> the cool, clear streams.
> Do you see this in your dreams?"
>
> "Love each other," he said to me,
> as I sat upon his knee.

That was before I even got my Indian name. And even in the deepest pain, when I couldn't really feel the beauty, I'd look at what the Creator had made, I'd look at the sky and I'd look at the trees and I'd look at the water and I'd look at the people and, like in the poem, sometimes I would feel like the Creator was there. And I knew, if He can make all this, He can help me through my pain.

When I put myself in treatment, that was the hardest time in my life and I started going to the sweat lodges a lot. I'd been to the sweats before but this time I really wanted to deal with forgiving the male abusers.

That's what I wanted to let go of at that time. And my spirit was in such pain. I never knew to let that go, to forgive would be so painful. I think if I had known it would hurt so much to let go of that ... It felt like it was coming from far far far away, I guess it's years and years and years, it was like a tree and when you pull it the roots are stuck in that ground and you are just pulling—that's the pain I felt inside, just like I was being pulled and pulled and pulled and ripped. I never felt physical pain like that before. But I knew it was spiritual pain. I was just moaning and it hurt. It hurt. It hurt.

I just kept going to the sweat lodges. It was a time when I really wanted to die but I didn't want to take my own life. I just kept hoping I'd have a heart attack or something.

I can remember the day when I finally came out of the sweat lodge, I don't know how many sweats I'd gone to, and I looked at the sky and there was just a gentle breeze across my face and I took a breath and I was just so happy to be alive. It was gone, that wanting to die. And I could see the beauty and I could see and feel the wind and really feel the love of the Creator.

But it still took time after that. I'd go through good times and then I'd go through hard, still digging, still looking. But I spent a lot of time affirming myself after that sweat. Looking for the good in me and wanting to let go of the hate—the hate I had for myself, for the kind of role model as a women I had shown my children. But there was a compassion for myself, a deeper understanding. I can't really blame my parents for what happened, I could start to see that. If I wanted to heal I couldn't really carry my hatred. But I could let myself get angry and not feel guilt. I used to feel a lot of guilt when I was angry at my mom.

I had to get rid of that hate. When I was around her there was always a part of me that wanted to say something, to be angry with her, rebel, or not really be warm. After I started really working on my feelings about my mom, I'd take out my picture album and look at her picture when she was fifteen and she was so beautiful, and I'd look at that picture and I'd cry and cry and cry. Because here was a woman who was so beautiful and she was pregnant with me when she was sixteen years old and my dad was twenty-four, and she got into an alcoholic relationship—a woman who never turned to alcohol for her pain. He was very violent and abusive to her, psychologically, physically and emotionally. And I came to understand that she had suffered. I'd look at that picture and cry. I don't know how many times I cried for that young girl, and I look at her and see how she is today. She can't even go outside the house, she is so scared of people. When we were growing up she'd say, "Don't tell people what goes on in this house. It's nobody's business."

And it shows me how, if you keep it in, you can go insane. You end up alone. She doesn't have a lot of friends, and my sisters and I don't visit her that often. You just grow old and there is no life inside you.

When I was going through my really hard times, I'd sit on the couch and I'd think of her. When I was sick and going through that pain, I'd think, "I don't want to be like her, I want to be okay. I want to be able to do things, I want to be able to talk. I want to share, I don't want to just sit in this living-room." That's what pushed me. I don't want to grow old when I'm still young. I don't want to end up like that.

I always prayed a lot, shared a lot with my friends. I started sharing with my children and I found out they were all sexually abused and that was really hard. When we moved out to the reserve they were raped and I didn't know that. I guess when I was going through my own healing, in the beginning, I never shared with them, and they were going through this by young guys.

That's part of the sickness, I guess. They say that if a parent is abused there is a good chance the children will be. Maybe it's because you have a passive personality or something. You don't really know how to fend for yourself and be assertive and your kids pick that up. I believe that's true.

And they saw me go through all kinds of abuse, including the ways I abused myself. It was hard, finding out my girls were also abused, because I knew that I could not make them heal. And I knew the pain that they were going to go through and I wanted to be able to go through it for them. I just had to pray that they would have the strength to go through what they had to go through. And I watched one of my daughters just vibrating on the bed once and her eyes looked like they were just going to come out of her from what she went through. She is twenty-two and she still doesn't get into relationships. I know there is still more there. She had two years of sobriety but she wasn't going to meetings. She told me that she went back to drinking. We are able to talk about it. That's one good thing. I am able to talk about things with my daughters and be understanding. She says, "I don't want to get back to the way I was before. I want to stop it before it gets bad."

I went through an eight-week therapy session a little while ago and I was told by the psychologist that what I have gone through in my life, even as a child, would have made most people insane or made them commit suicide by the time they were teenagers. She said there is something very powerful in me. She said I scared her when we met because I knew more than her. She said I was hurt in every cell of my being, in all ways a child can be hurt, and yet there was something special in me that kept me going.

I remember as a little girl thinking of a little fire in me, a little light. And even through all those hard, hard times I would always think about that little light. That little light was never squashed. Maybe I got that from church when I was a little girl: "This little light of mine—I'm going to let it shine."

♦

We had a human sexuality expert do a workshop on the reserve and what he found out was that about eighty-five percent of the people at the workshop had been abused or were abusers. Some of us at that workshop decided to form a team and we brought the same leader back to give us training in human sexuality. After that we started survivor meetings in the open. We shared our stories in the school and with community leaders. We were out in the open now. And then some of the men started sharing too, either that they were abused or abusers. So nothing surprises me anymore, I've heard so much, about so many ways that people are hurt. It is hard to listen to because you get weak.

We hold workshops to educate and make the public accept that this kind of abuse is happening, and to make it possible for the young girls and boys to come forward if they are being abused, so that we can stop it. And that is the reason that I have started speaking openly. I want a safe place for my grandchildren. I have a little granddaughter and she was there when we lived on the reserve. I thought, I was abused, my daughters were abused, but my granddaughter? I wanted a safe place for her and if it was out in the open and not secret, kids could be educated about what abuse is, and they could start dealing with their issues when they are young and not have to go through it as adults or teenagers.

♦

When I started working with them, a lot of women didn't even know that it was abuse—to be fondled. They couldn't understand why they couldn't really enjoy sex, why they would want to push their husband's or boyfriend's hand away. They didn't know how much being raped or even touched can hurt your spirit. And how it can affect your life and hurt you over and over and over because you are so ashamed. Hopefully, now, some of those young children can talk and it can be out in the open.

II

re-imagining faith, re-imagining the world

body imagery

Yvette

"
I do not have many safe places and I'm trying to extend the number of safe places I have. It's not so much physical safety, it's more who has access to me when I'm in a vulnerable position, like when I sleep. I have trouble on airplanes because I don't feel safe in enclosed spaces. When I travelled overseas I would find that men would molest me on an airplane and I would not have the power to say no. Not awful molestation, but I would still feel deprived of my dignity if they put their hand on my thigh when they thought I was sleeping, and of course I'd pretend to sleep. I've only acquired the power lately to believe that I don't have to submit to that. A couple of times I was able to protect myself by moving to another seat, but it took all my energy to believe that I could, because I would think I was going to hurt him if I moved to another seat. This is a terrible distortion of what is important. So I still have a hard time knowing what my boundaries are. And I have a hard time believing that his whims, whoever he is, are not superior to my need for privacy and boundaries. It's just so stupid, it feels so stupid, I feel so indignant. I imagine myself scum and not able to do anything—totally paralysed. It is very hard to imagine taking steps to make myself safe, even now.

I think I reverted to a childhood feeling that by my very existence as a female I provoke men to molest me. I'm responsible. So I should just fade into the woodwork or something. I connect these feelings not only with my childhood, but with the socialization of all women, with advertising, and with pornography. If I scream, I'm the one to blame because I'm the one with the female body and everyone will accept the molestation as normal. I revert back. Mentally I know I can change that, but my body doesn't seem to know it.

But it is coming. I am hopeful. I am taking quiet time this summer. It is the first summer in my whole life when I haven't had to do extra jobs. I'm on sabbatical and working part-time. I am taking time to read and walk and pray, although not in the conventional way.

It's not safe to have a male God anymore. I call "Him" a bully, rapist God and I have a female Goddess now. I still want a personal relationship with God so I guess I still hang on to a God that has personal qualities.

I think that, say in a black society like South Africa, where I worked for twenty years, the image of a strong warrior God is what they need to believe so that they can stand up against oppression. And I think that is probably what happened in early patriarchy. In order to survive the cultures around them, the Christians needed a powerful, almighty God and that has come through as the standard way we view God, and that, in turn, shapes how we view the world and the use of power in the world. There are other images of God in the Bible, which have not been read in churches—images like the mother hen who collects her chicks. The womb is a very powerful image throughout the Old Testament, but it has been ignored.

I am re-imagining my faith and fortunately there are other women and men around who are doing the same thing and that gives me hope. Women sometimes need to imagine an all-powerful warrior God and see themselves as warriors in order to fight and transform the oppression in their own lives and then in the wider culture.

In order to imagine a different world, I am reading only what women write, and only the writing of women who are aware. I just won't read a book by a man for the time being.

I am beginning to believe in women. I am reading women's interpretation of scripture and it is changing the whole thing. I am beginning to believe women were there all the time, but were silenced. Before, I couldn't imagine women being there, thinking and doing.

I knew for years that I would be radical someday, but I didn't have the courage back then, I didn't quite believe. I was certainly a feminist but I didn't have enough information. There was so little support for what I was thinking. I would put things on hold and I'd do my little bits, but I'd shake when I'd say things that I knew would go against the grain. And then I was in another culture and I thought, why am I trying to touch their culture? I'd better go back to my own culture.

When I came back to my own culture I found myself feeling so angry. The pain got so bad. I don't even think it was the incest, I think it's the whole condition of women. But it *was* the incest—and it wasn't even really severe for me. It was normal, in a sense, for me. It was the condition of women in my family, and the dysfunction, that was so awful. The molestation was minimal, it was the attitude that was so devastating. I can only imagine what it is like for women who are raped in childhood. A number of women who have come to see me have been molested from the age of two and younger. From birth, practically.

I think my pain is becoming a gift in that I am beginning to be able to imagine a different world, partly through believing that my body has messages, that how I viewed the world before isn't how God wanted it, it isn't what creation is about. I can't imagine changing the world very much but I can imagine fighting for it, and it is worth fighting for.

I imagined women's lives, but I never imagined how bad it was. For me it was just normal. The word for women and the word for slave are identical in one Egyptian hieroglyphic. In fact, in the United States the definitive book on slavery was published in 1902 and it said that slavery just doesn't exist as long as only women are involved. So it was the normal condition and I was used to "normal," until I could imagine that it didn't have to be like that ... breaking traditions is such a hard thing to do, and anyone who tries will be condemned for trying.

I think God is bigger than what we have imagined the church to be. I don't think the church we have now was what Jesus planned. I don't fit into the official church very well. Maybe I'm holding onto it for other reasons, and maybe that is what most people do. Jesus really gives me hope because he didn't discriminate. Slavery and women were so intertwined. We have worked a little bit at slavery, but very little. Externally we have eliminated slavery but not internally and not even in social customs. And I think it is the same with women.

When I look at the subject of faith, and its role in healing from incest and sexual abuse, I worry about the kind of faith that says "let go." I do have to let go of certain things but I also have to take charge of others. For me it has been trying to find a balance in faith: letting go of what has been distorted and taking charge of my rights, which are more than just selfish rights, they are the rights to be human, to be free, to be alive. And I think Jesus did that. But when I hear faith defined as "let go and let God" I get really worried. It depends on what a person means by letting go. Even letting go of the anger—so I can be peaceful? So that I can be abused again? That is my sense of my past: I was peaceful, I was submissive, whatever, to keep the peace. And all it got me was abuse or permission for the others to abuse me. So I am very careful about words or concepts like that.

Last week a woman was saying that maybe I expect too much of myself. But if we are created we should be able to expect a full life, not a life that is pushed down and limited. As if I'm limited to the jobs women do in the church—sitting in the pew, not at the altar. So we went through a whole discussion of, "Why are we taught to expect less?" And I don't think that is what religion should be all about but I think that is what religion has done. But it hasn't done it only to women, it has done it to the poor classes, the native population and blacks. Often I think the message of the Christian church has been interpreted as, "Accept that you are lesser, don't demand too much because you won't get it." Well, that may be a practical viewpoint, but I don't think that is what faith is all about. So I have great hope. I know I don't understand my faith very well. It is exciting to see whole new interpretations of it. It really is exciting. I know faith has always been important.

I am working toward a faith that will allow me to truly feel alive rather than to limit me. My abuse as a child was so small, and yet it had such an impact on my faith. My father fondled my breasts in public when I was developing. I was ten, eleven, or twelve. His statement was, in Flemish, "She will be a big-breasted wife for some lucky man." Of course that was the expectation in that milieu. But my twin brother was going to be a lawyer or a priest. And that has always stuck with me—the low expectations for women. All they can do is please some man. This is where letting go comes in. I will let go of that image and take charge of my image, of what I am really meant to be. I am not to be defined by outside forces.

I believe that my body was marvellously created, is good, has messages in it. And I believe that imagery comes through the body—that I can imagine fullness. I am full of ideas about life, about what women can do, and that men don't need to be batterers, that the myth we have lived with, of man's dominance and woman's subservience, is no longer valid. The imagery of the new myth is much more one of partnership.

But it sobers me to realize that in fifty years, with all the corrections that feminism might make, what I think is the ideal now will have distortions in it. The image of partnership, for instance, isn't going to be perfect for everyone in the future. Just as God the Father was the perfect image for some people at some time, but it is now dysfunctional for a good number of us. And God the Mother isn't much better. I think I need God to have a lot of images. I think it is idolatry to have only one image of God.

I grew up thinking that if I took power I would be out of control and I'd be destructive. And that's probably not true. Responsibility does come, or should come, with more power.

My religion shouldn't have been something that limited my ability, but how could I imaginine it not to be, when I look at how it was interpretated to me? I feel like I'm a late bloomer but I am going to bloom. I kind of resent the years that I have dawdled along. I don't resent what I did, because I enjoyed the stuff I was doing. I just keep wondering how I can integrate it all in the next few years so that I can have an impact on myself and maybe on others.

I have been too angry in the last few years. I didn't have enough information—I would use emotion rather than information because I still did not have enough imagery and history. I still don't feel I have enough of that to be calm. I'm not yet convinced that I have rights. But it is coming, I notice a big difference in myself in the last two years. I feel more self-possessed and if somebody challenges me, I have information that I can give them instead of attacking them or crying.

I have an example from when I was living in Chicago. There were four of us living together and at breakfast this woman from New Zealand said,

"Didn't Patricia give a good talk yesterday?" Patricia, a Benedictine nun, had given a wonderful talk. But then the New Zealand woman added, "She talks like a man!" Within seconds my hands were clenched, I was standing up and tears were rolling down. Obviously, they picked up on the fact that I was upset and we were able to discuss it. But, I was so upset ... my body had the reaction before my head was all there. So I am beginning to trust that when my body reacts, there is something wrong. It was a new thing to me, my body reaction—before, I would have let it go. I am no longer willing to let it go, but I am not good at knowing exactly how to react—I still over-reacted. But it was okay because the New Zealand woman was able to say, "Why should a woman have to be like a man to give a good talk? She was not like a man, she was like Pat!" And that helped me to believe in myself and in my body. That kind of thing has given me faith that when there is a gut reaction or a body reaction, it is because my body has something to say, that there is something wrong about the image or situation. And I wait for my body to tell me what it is.

One of the things I do for myself is to stand in front of a mirror naked and look at myself and talk to the different parts of my body, starting with my feet, to find out what message they have. I've done that every day for a week.

Another exercise I do is to pick a part of my body that I like very much and then have a dialogue with it about how it feels, what it has to say. And then I enlarge upon that the next day, talking not just to that part but to the area around it, eventually taking in the whole body.

I often try to imagine myself as walking tall. It is a simple thing, but for me there is so much self-imagery involved. Positive self-imagery was knocked out of me and out of my brothers as well. I think I got a bigger dose of it as a female, but children, male or female, weren't valued in my family. For me, walking tall represents dignity and self-possession.

"

♦

Yvette still belongs to a religious order. She has a new job running government training programs. "My first assignment was setting up a project to deal with sexual abuse in a rural community," she says. "I had to pull together a lot of information, do a lot of reading, and self-searching. I realized I have a lot more rights than I ever believed or allowed myself ... I have always felt slotted into a very narrow existence because of being a woman. I always felt I had to be dependent and ask permission of a higher authority—a man, or the ultimate authority, the church—to do anything. It seems so silly now ... I can't cope with the formal church anymore, even though I still belong to a religious order. I can't even walk into a church. I don't know how I'm going to resolve that problem!"

united yet unique

Alexis D'Amour

"   In the past three years my struggle to
achieve wholeness has opened up to me the world of self-help meetings, individual and group therapy, books and other material pertaining to adult
children of alcoholics, abused women, and women survivors of child abuse.
I have heard and read about others who experience the pain, the fear, the
hurt, the humiliation, the shame and the guilt similar to my own. I am not
alone—our numbers are untold. There are many who are still afraid to tell
their story. Those of us who have found the strength and the courage to
trust another human being—one who accepts us as we are—discover a
bond with other survivors.

Yes, I know I am united with those who understand my sufferings, and
yet, I feel alone. In my isolation I become confused. Or does my confusion
cause me to feel isolated? Whichever it may be, it makes no difference. I still
feel different from other survivors. In my research I have yet to come across
another individual who, like myself, carries one additional burden to those
previously mentioned—the burden of living with a physical disability from
the time of birth.

Denial regarding the abuse of children is common in our society, as common as the abuse itself. If people find it so difficult to accept the existence of
child abuse in our so-called average families, this denial escalates when we
speak about the abuse of a child who has a disability. We must reach out to
these individuals, help them to emerge from their world of darkness into
the safety of a loving, accepting, understanding environment. Individuals
with disabilities are united with other survivors, yet we are unique.

Children are dependent on adults for the necessities of life. How much
greater are the needs of a child with a disability! I was raped at the age of six
after requesting assistance to go to the toilet. I was totally dependent upon
others for the basics of life, which are so often taken for granted. Unable to
even walk, where could I "run?" Due to my uncontrollable movements and
slurred speech, I am commonly treated as a being with no intellect. If this is
so in my adult years, who would ever listen to a child with these difficulties?

After a lifetime of being misunderstood and rejected, I was afraid to reach out for the help I so desperately needed. Yet when I did, I found there are people willing to listen to me and to accept the person within this spastic body. As I continue my journey towards wholeness, there are times when the fear is still greater than my longing to be healed, but I must overcome the temptation to retreat into the darkness. I believe there is a light waiting to renew my being. With the caring support of the people around me, I have the strength and the courage to reach it. There are many women with disabilities who are survivors of child abuse. They are hiding in their own world of silence. My prayer is that, somewhere along the way, I will meet these women. Then I will truly know that I am not alone.

"

♦

"I left home and became involved in a difficult marriage. I finally got the strength to go out on my own four years ago. Despite serious health complications, I am pursuing a career as an artist and have had my work shown in a major Canadian gallery."

who am I?

highlights of my struggle for identity

Amy

"

The question "Who am I?" is one which has always bothered me. It would give me the feeling that everyone else knew a secret which I was excluded from knowing. My life had conditioned me to focus always upon everyone else, doing my best to avoid being hurt. I never looked at me, nor was I encouraged to do so. On the contrary, the emphasis from family, community, churches and career was always on being other-centred, which just came naturally to me. Unfortunately, in my own perception of myself this other-centred being was still a non-person. As a child I learned that I had to be pretty and thin and cooperative if I was to get any of the attention that I craved. Today I still battle with these first learnings. My identity is no longer so totally involved with the physical, but I am aware of its influence. The child in me needs lots of reassurance from me concerning this. The struggle is to love parts of me that have been so hurt, so used and abused.

Early in my recovery process, my sense of self was all tied up with my woundedness, with my pain. My pain brought me people to help me, to listen to me, and I have been afraid to let go of this. I thought I wouldn't be loved if I got better, because the only time I was attended to was when I was in pain.

My journey to find out who I am led me to books and study, to meetings, courses and sessions, to people. Very slowly I have moved from identifying myself with negatives, with sickness, with sexual object, with inferior being, with nothing, to believing I have some small value and, later, some greater value. In short I became a somebody.

Study led me to the belief that at the centre of me was love, and one day I came to experience that love, to feel it inside me. However, I was not immediately able to identify this experience of love in me as myself, to own this gift. It took time to quell the negative voices in me, to strengthen the positive ones.

It is taking a lifetime to try to practise in all my daily experiences the love I know I have within me. I fail to love very often but life seems to continually invite me to keep trying to be willing to accept my failures and mistakes and weariness and frustration and resentment and start each day as just that, a new day.

Often, in my confusion over identity, I would struggle with the notions of womanhood until I realized I could form my own and decide for myself.

A group session at WPTC helped me to become more conscious of who I am by expanding my idea of self to include my values, ideas, hopes and attitudes, and not to limit my self-concept to an earlier view. It helped me to celebrate how I express and nurture what I believe to be the essence of me.

I still feel hurt and pain and fear when the words "creative," "talents" and "imagination" are in the air and I often cry over them. I see I still have shame. Today my positive identity (the new me) manages to cope with the negative (the old me) side of myself quite successfully most of the time.

In my recovery process, I have made many mistakes in relationships, and learned from these mistakes. At one point, I became involved in an abusive relationship with a priest. I met the priest at a workshop. He offered to see me after it was over. He said he figured I needed a lot of help. My emotions were frozen at the time. He said, "You haven't had enough love." He said that psychiatrists don't "finish the job."

After we had met a few times, he started holding and hugging me, and it brought back a lot of feelings. I was naive. I thought all priests did this when counselling. And I felt cared about, which was a new feeling.

He was an alcoholic, although I didn't realize it right away. In time, I began to question our relationship. When I realized he was an alcoholic and confronted him, he made excuses. Meanwhile I was feeling all this stuff I had never felt before. He was giving me all sorts of warmth and attention. I was hooked. It progressed from there to "sex for healing." In his view, "sex for sex" was not okay, but "sex for healing" was okay.

I was caught—I was emotionally engaged, but it was father-daughter stuff, not a relationship of equals. He was the counsellor and he betrayed my trust, and the vulnerability that had brought me to him in the first place. After it got bad, the little girl in me was scared and I had trouble leaving. The woman in me wasn't strong enough. I am an adult child of an alcoholic and a survivor of incest—and here I was in a parallel situation, involved with a "Father" of the Church who was sworn to celibacy. This was yet another taboo, another secret for which I had to bear the emotional load and shame.

Eventually, I walked out. He was drinking a lot more and I wasn't getting any help. I was helping him, listening to his concerns and problems. His needs had become paramount.

I went through hell after that. For years I blamed myself.

Another mistake I made was to too freely discuss my past with people (such as neighbours) who were either not strong enough to contain the information or were totally frightened by what I revealed to them. My intention in telling them about myself was to form a relationship. It had worked in therapy and I tried to use the method of disclosure on everybody, thinking that I would make friends, that, indeed, this is how one goes about making real friends. It had some sad results in my personal life. So I learned discretion, and that my relationships, in their early stages at least, do not require my entire life history. They depend only on me and who I am today, and the other person and who that person is today, and what we have to share.

portrait of a friendship

I met my friend when I was thiry-five. The year before, I had fallen into a severe depression after coming off anti-depressants when pregnant with my second child, and was hospitalized. In a magic moment, waiting for electrodes placed at my temples to scatter my thoughts to the four winds, I experienced a moment of truth, a rebirth. It unlocked the doors that had been frozen shut for so very long. Soon after I met my friend, who has walked beside me with such fidelity and strength and honesty that I can only wonder at my great fortune.

By this time I had been free of addictions for about five years and I stayed away from anti-depressants. I was just barely beginning to have a sense of self and I believed I was loved by God and that I needed new parents. I especially felt the need for a mother—that was what was drawing me to my friend.

At first I was scared of her. I felt she wouldn't want to know me. I saw her at intervals and it took me awhile to piece it together. I slowly realized that was what I wanted—for her to mother me. It took all my courage but I phoned her and asked her. At first she was a little leery—she had several grown children. But we got together within a few days and spent the whole morning together. As soon as we got together all the old stuff came up.

I began to thaw, to feel, to warm in the atmosphere of safety and strength and honesty with which my friend provided me. I possessed over thirty years of unlived life, and the memories of neglect and sexual abuse I had experienced as a child began to surface and demand recognition.

In the presence of my friend's love and with the support of others, I expressed all the non-love that I had known needed to be expressed.

At various times in my recovery, I have also received help from professionals—some good and some very harmful to me. I see that the impact of sexual abuse and alcoholism in the family I was born into were literally ignored by many, and some pieces of the puzzle of my life were not allowed to be discovered until so much time had passed. My pattern of being controlled by my need for my father's love, and his abuse of me, set me up to be abused by other male authority figures. It was not until I became conscious of the little girl in me that I was able to dismantle this terrible cycle of pain and unmet need. I tried to pattern the re-parenting of my inner child after the parenting I received from my friend.

Following a particularly bad experience with a helping professional, I found it very difficult to seek any further help and for several years I just wanted to stay with my friend. But eventually and thankfully, I did arrive at the door of the WPTC where some important aspects of my recovery have finally been addressed, and where I have met others who have had similar experiences and with whom I have been able to share my journey.

I still see my friend and we talk at least once a week and I am trying to take my full place in the relationship. I have needed her so much. No words can give sufficient tribute to her and the love she has for me. I thank her for who she is and for helping me to become myself. Of all the people I have met, she is the person I would most hope to be like. She is a gracious human being.

"

♦

Amy is married and has two children. "Gardening, walking, nature ... just being outdoors makes me happy. Having been in the business of recovery for twenty years, I want people who have gone through similar experiences to have access to material and help that wasn't available to me. I think how different it would have been for me if twenty years ago the psychiatrist had said, 'This agency can help you.'

"A lot of my burden was swept under the rug and I had to carry it with me. It distorts your whole presence in the world. You are not the person you might be. I have regrets that my children didn't have access to parts of me that they might have had when they were young. So I have been working to make it different for survivors now. Over the fifteen years I actively struggled alone with my history, no one said to me, 'Look Amy, you are programmed to be abused!' Then I would have known to be careful, and the priest would not have been able to abuse me.

"The psychiatrist did nothing with the information that I had been sexually and emotionally abused. His concern was, 'Are you going to A.A. meetings?' As soon as I got information about the impact of abuse, and someone was willing and able to work with me, my life moved ahead."

a friend's story

Amy's friend

"

I am writing this from the perspective of a non-professional, who acted as a support person for a period of fifteen years. Amy had already begun her journey of self-discovery when I met her.

As I reflect on the growth of the relationship between us over those years, I see my role as one of listener, friend, receiver of pain, encourager and occasionally, counsellor.

The journey of healing on which we embarked was one of mutual learning about pain, feelings of worthlessness, abandonment, anger, betrayal and eventually, the discovery of inner strength, confidence and self-respect.

As we began our relationship, Amy and I met on a weekly basis. She phoned at least once a day between meetings, sometimes more often if a particularly painful episode was being relived. Over the years our contacts became less frequent, according to need. We still keep in contact by phone about once a week, to maintain our connectedness.

Throughout these years my respect for Amy has been constant and I have been inspired by her courage. She took the responsibility for her own healing and I trusted her own innate wisdom to discover within herself the path to growth and wholeness. It was necessary for us to have an abundance of patience because the road to health has been a long one which has taken many years. We now know that growth is a never-ending process.

We learned together that the pain is evacuated in stages. Pain-filled situations were faced and relived. Through that process we gained new insights, and my friend's self-confidence was strengthened. At a later time we noticed that the same situation, or a similar situation, would surface again and would have to be confronted once more. However, the pain was evacuated with the strength gained from the previous experience. Depending upon the depth of the pain, that process was repeated several times in some aspects of her life.

For some time in our relationship, Amy cast me in the role of counsellor. Over the years, if a breakthrough was made to equal the relationship, she was quick to put herself back into the role of someone needing help rather than finding her role in a friendship of equals. Although that was somewhat frustrating, I accepted that, and allowed her to move at her own speed. Eventually I brought that observation to her attention, but allowed her to choose the timing for change. After a long period, we related as equals more frequently.

Along the way, I was aware that there were areas of my friend's life history which required professional help. For instance, I could receive her anger but I did not have the expertise to facilitate expression of that anger in non-destructive ways. She sought out that help for herself as she did in other areas needing professional attention.

As our journey progressed it was often necessary to help Amy to determine if feelings arising from a disturbing situation from the past were clouding her perception, reactions or actions. If so, we dealt with the old feelings and then took a new look at what triggered them to determine how to deal with the present situation in a more appropriate manner. This was not always easy. A lot of growing had to take place before the realization was made that one is responsible for one's own feelings and the response to them.

Amy entered university and grew tremendously through study, interaction with others, exploring her many intellectual gifts and earning a degree.

As my friend was making such great strides there were times when she would get so caught up in the vicissitudes of her external life that she would forget to draw on her inner strength and wisdom. Anxiety and self-doubt would inevitably creep in. My role was to encourage her to look within herself, to remember how far she had come, to remind her of past accomplishments and cheer her on.

Sometimes I felt uncomfortable when it appeared that I was a role model for my friend because I knew my own faults and weaknesses and often considered her to be much more courageous and insightful than myself.

There were many occasions when I had to draw on my deep faith that God meant for each one of us to realize our full potential as human beings. As long as my friend was seeking wholeness and courageously entering into her own healing, I knew she would eventually emerge victorious. Because of that I could remain relatively peaceful when she embarked on a road which seemed to contain potential stumbling blocks. My role was to allow her the room to experiment and explore without censor.

I do not know whether Amy can yet fully appreciate her life history but I highly value it because it has made her who she is today, a person I cherish for her perception, caring, courage, dignity and friendship.

Over the years Amy has slowly moved from having a self-image as a victim to being a survivor. I shall rejoice when she clearly sees herself as a person with deep inner beauty and strength, a warrior queen victorious.

"

partner

Leon

"
According to current statistics, one in four females will experience some form of sexual abuse. What the statistics don't take into account is the fact that many of these victims go on to have relationships with other people. In the process of trying to get on with life, some marry and have children. It's within this category that I find myself, the significant other. I met Shelley in high school while I was completing my grade twelve. We eloped shortly after school and have been together for almost seventeen years.

I won't go into the details of our married life. It was normal under the circumstances—we both came from abusive homes. I will say that the dynamics of modern relationships are demanding in themselves, and Shelley and I experienced a lot of hardships but maintained our marriage.

Almost four years ago I found out some horrible things had happened to Shelley when she was growing up. I knew about her father. He used to drink with my grandfather and my uncles, so I knew about the alcoholism in her background. I also knew that with the alcoholism came a degree of violence and mental abuse.

What I didn't know about was the sexual abuse. This came out four years ago when we returned to Winnipeg so I could attend university.

Our relationship began to deteriorate almost as soon as we got here. Shelley is a strong woman and she tried her best to maintain our relationship. The worst part started in the winter. Shelley was always a little high strung, but something was different. We would argue almost all the time now and she would run away. She was running from something. I thought maybe it was me.

It wasn't until an incident where she ran to the bus depot that I stopped feeling sorry for myself for the loss of my wife, that I stepped out of my role as husband. At that point I wanted to know the answer and I remembered something my psychology professor said in a lecture. I listened to what she was saying. This is when I became deeply involved with what was happening to her. I had to ignore my own feelings of loss and step outside of my emotional dependency. This is probably the first time in a long time that I actually listened to what she was saying. What she was saying was, "I'm going to die" and she was terrified. Just as terrified as if someone was holding a gun to her head.

– ‖ –

The things that my wife related to me were horrible and disgusting. I never knew people could be so inhuman. The first incident was when she was eight years old. I knew the people she spoke of. Some of them were my relatives and what she told me was not beyond belief, but it was horrible.

I felt a sense of bewilderment and outrage. When you become involved with a person, you become involved with the continuity of that individual's life. I feel what she went through just as if it happened yesterday. As a close person, you are not afforded the protection of the therapist. The therapist gets to go home after dealing with the patient. For me, home became an uncertainty. Is she there? Is she okay? Will I find her at the bus depot again? Or maybe hiding under the table like a terrified animal? Maybe she'll be angry and again I will become those terrible men, or represent my sex as a target for the rage and hostility.

Sometimes it would be nice. I would find her in a pleasant but aloof mood and we would go to sleep without war, anxiety or terror.

The pleasant times made it hard. I knew how much effort it took to get back to the point where Shelley could be calm. Sometimes we were so close to each other that I would want to die, so I would never feel any other emotion again. It was in one of those periods that Shelley asked me never to leave her no matter what and most of all not to let anyone put her in an institution. I kept my promise. I watched over her treatment and developed a trust in her therapist.

The anger grew inside her. It slowly consumed the woman I knew. As she gave into her anger more and more, I lost hope. I found myself numb. Like the tin man, I could not feel anymore and I wondered if I ever would again.

I felt alone for the first time in my life. My family was no help. They hated Shelley and would have been glad if I left her. In desperation, I found myself a mistress. I know I have no excuses for that and I regret involving someone else in something I should have handled myself.

You see, there are no services for the significant other. No one you can go to and talk to, no sense of companionship or community. It's like you are by yourself in deep space, removed from society because of the terrible things you have witnessed through the victim. You become a secondary victim and soon you develop the tough outer shell to protect your sensibilities.

I felt all the rage and the outrage. I felt the horror almost beyond belief. I have witnessed humanity at its worst. It was like crawling through the sewers, or much like Dante going into the pit of Hell.

Today I have still not recovered from my journey. It might take some time before I can deal with all that I saw Shelley go through. My perspective on the world has changed drastically and I am still angry at the loss. It's like someone murdered Shelley. In a way they did—I watched her die.

– III –

There is a positive side to all of this, because out of the death of Shelley rose the phoenix Shelley. From the ashes of a charred and ruined past came the woman who I now live with. I was the one who first used the phoenix as a symbol for Shelley because that's what I expected from someone as strong as her.

The cost has been high for both Shelley and myself and the demands placed on the therapists were incredible. But it worked. Shelley is once again a strong independent woman. She is more in control and is far more relaxed than I have ever seen her. She is like a new person and I guess she is.

As for myself, dealing with what happened to Shelley has caused me to look at what has happened to me. It caused me to re-evaluate myself and the role I have had for myself. I too am going through my phoenix-like transition.

I know that some of what I have written may not be what one would want to hear. There was no way to maintain the honesty and integrity without laying down the bare facts. During the last four years I have had to deal with things I don't like, but that's life.

My advice to anyone involved with an incest or sexual abuse victim is to stick with it. The final result can be worth the cost. My only regret is the fact that there are no services available to men who are involved with survivors of incest. The survivor is a difficult person to deal with if you don't understand what she is going through. Now I realize that I can know, in an intellectual way, but I can never feel, what it was like to be in that position.

I would like to thank all those who helped me by teaching me to listen, showing me what to listen to, showing me how to deal with what I had to listen to, and telling me to get up and do something about it. And to Shelley—thanks for giving me the courage.

"

♦

Leon is a thirty-four-year-old Cree Indian. "My identity was denied me during my growing up years. I've gone through many changes, and many are related to Shelley's personal walk. This has changed the way I see things and helped me clarify my direction for myself. I started looking at not just the surface of the water—but much deeper."

a gay partner's story

Sheillah

"

When I first met my partner, she was quite vague about her background. She said that her childhood was pretty horrendous and that she really hated her step-father, who was an alcoholic. Eventually, she talked about an incident that took place when she was about nine. She didn't describe what had happened, but she talked about how she had felt afterward. Gradually, she talked more, but not much more. It was very difficult for her.

I didn't want to be her counsellor, so I tried not to probe too much. But it really did affect our relationship. There were a lot of similarities between this woman and me. I am a survivor of incestuous sexual abuse myself. I am also employed as a social worker and it didn't take me long to figure our that she had been sexually abused.

I was in counselling when the relationship began. My relationship with my partner made me look at my tendency to get hooked into relationships where I play the caretaker role. Recently, I've done a lot of work on that, on not caretaking in a number of areas of my life.

Gradually, I began to realize that my partner had a major drinking problem, too. When I met her, she told me she had a drinking problem. Six months into the relationship, she admitted she was an alcoholic. It caused a lot of problems.

I know a lot about alcoholism. I grew up in an alcoholic family. My father was an alcoholic and I often work with alcoholics through my job. When my partner got treatment for her alcoholism, I had great hopes for her. She started communicating quite honestly with me, and she went into counselling for her incest issues. I really felt she was making great strides, after thirty years of never talking about it.

But I could never give enough to her. She was very demanding and extremely jealous. She took up all my time and space and she was angry at me a lot because I couldn't be there for her constantly. She was asking me to fill up all the empty spaces, to be there all the time, to be her parent.

180

This relationship forced me to look at my own self and where I was. It was the fourth in a series of relationships that had been very destructive to me. I was the caretaker in my family, I've been the overbearing mother (I have two children), I've been everybody's social worker and I do it for a living. This relationship really forced me to look at why I get hooked into pain, and to question whether I confuse love and pity.

This relationship really caused me to examine my own fears of abandonment. Everytime my partner ran off, I would think, "There is something wrong with me, I'm not giving enough." So then I'd go through this cycle where I'd double my efforts to be there emotionally, and I'd be exhausted.

That's how it works with me. I simply don't get my needs met so I burn out and get tired and frustrated and when total exhaustion comes, I quit the relationship. And by then it feels kind of ugly.

I ended my relationship with my partner a month ago, and I feel guilty. I don't want to feel guilty, but I do. She is in incredible pain and phones me a lot. When I stop and think about it, and feel how much I care about her, I feel very badly.

But for now I plan to do some of my own work, on my own issues, and not get involved for awhile. And I'm really going to go slow if I do meet someone. I'm not saying that I'll never become involved with a woman who is an incest survivor. That would be ridiculous. But, the woman would have to have done some work on recovering from the incest, and not expect me to be a parent. She would also have to be honest and open and say the word, "incest." I know I have a lot of work left to do myself. I grew up equating caring with self-sacrifice. I've never quite figured out how else to care.

I don't expect to be with someone who has it all figured out and had got it all together. I just expect someone who can talk about things, who knows she has buttons and can communicate when they have been pressed, and who has a middle ground between screaming and running away. Someone who believes its okay for me to be angry sometimes too—who isn't threatened by that.

"

♦

"In the year that has passed since the writing of my story, my partner and I tried a few more times to keep our relationship together. Finally, and painfully, I admitted to myself that it was a destructive relationship. I am continuing to work on my own healing process."

after therapy

M.J.

"

I went into therapy more than three years ago—a while after my dad had died and my marriage had broken up. My dad was an alcoholic and a batterer. My mom had stayed with him for eighteen years because she just couldn't face being on her own—she was unable to find the courage.

From my mother I learned fear and dependency. I also learned that a woman is supposed to do what the man wants.

When I left my husband the first time, after a lot of abuse, my mom pushed me to go back to him. The second time we split up I didn't look to anyone else. I just let him go.

My mother, sisters and brothers are all still going through a bad time. My mom never "outgrew" her own mother. After my dad died in 1985, our family really split up and went separate ways. We quit pretending that we were a happy family. I decided a few years ago that for our family to be happy was an impossible dream. This was an important and freeing decision. My family is still blood family to me but my brothers and sisters and I are stuck with being just siblings, not friends. I've accepted this.

The therapy seems a very long time ago now, but the abuse has never been buried. It still seems close whenever I talk with someone in my family.

I was pushing myself from the inside long before entering therapy. The therapy was only part of my healing process. Another part was deciding that people had to accept me as I am—that I had as much right to like myself as anyone else.

At that stage, I was still very dependent. I needed someone to depend on as I got through the pain. I knew I couldn't run from it. I had to face it. But I'd never had a parent who cared and I really needed someone. So, I had to figure out how to parent myself. I used to picture myself as a little girl in God's arms. I'd never really been held and this really helped.

People are often afraid of therapy—afraid of the pain. There was pain. I'd hurt and go home after sessions and cry, but it was good to be able to cry.

I'll never forget how important it was to meet others who cried for the same reasons. I remember listening to them. I could never sit and talk with my mother and sisters like that. I still think of those women and see their faces and feel that closeness—like sisters but more than sisters. My sisters put up fences. They still do this. Even friends have their own private lives. In therapy we were so close. It was really different and I learned about trust. It brought openness. There were no fences.

Since that time I've gone back to school and now I'm working in a non-traditional job. It is going well—I enjoy it and I'm good at it.

I don't depend on other peoples' opinions of me now. I'm different, happier, I laugh a lot and do lots of "crazy" things. I have a little puppy and I take her for long walks. I never would have done that five years ago. I feel so much freedom now. I take a lot of risks.

I work largely with men and I still don't relax too much around men. I'm pretty serious at work. I've seen too many "giggly women." I do not want to be thought of as another "tits and ass," just me.

Family to me now are my sons and a caring partner. I don't lead the kind of life I ever imagined I would. When I was a child I was so fearful and dependent, always afraid of losing my mom. Then in my marriage I was afraid of being without my husband. Now I don't have fears like those. I know that life goes on and the holes fill in. I found this out by cutting my husband out of my life and facing the fear and unknown.

After my husband and I separated, I saw myself as never entering another relationship. I pictured myself as only having ties to my children. I'd have lots of hobbies; a single "old" lady. I never imagined that I'd be open to another relationship. My present relationship is a long-standing one but it's not obsessive and it's not a "fear thing." I'm not afraid of the future and I'm always myself without any hidden secrets.

I'm different now, too, in that I don't want revenge anymore on my ex-husband. I did for a long time. Now I feel some pity for him. I never thought I'd be healthy. I thought I'd still be doubting my sanity. My ex-husband regularly threatened me with drives to the mental hospital and with comments about my mental health. I had done several stints in psychiatric wards and I could have used that as a crutch for a long time. I'm glad I didn't.

I used to get suicidal. There was a time when I spent many hours in closets—sometimes with a belt around my neck. It's not like that anymore. I never feel that way now.

When I think of the future I still want to do so much more. I want to meet more people. I want to tantalize people with my talents. I want to stir them up and say something *for women*—not against men. As women we all have winds inside of us and we are blown every which way. Men are told to look to themselves. As women, we've been told not to go against the men. Look to the man. But I've always been one not to follow the traditional. I wanted my life to be *my* life, and to look to myself.

Being a survivor isn't everything, but I've also found that there is no satisfaction in hurting back. I've done that too—been just as destructive as the men in my life. Now I just want to have a safe place. I don't want to walk around in men's clothes, or apologize for being a woman. I just want to be a person. I think I'm in the process of hatching a book but I've got a lot more reading to do before I write it. The book would not be a therapy book, but it would be about women's inner conflict.

In the future I may get married again. I hope to get an English degree. I want very much to be a grandmother—a good grandmother, not like mine. There were too many lies when I was growing up. I never again want to base any relationship with anyone on lies. Another surprise is that I find it hard to lie now. I'm not sure where that came from because I grew up lying—having to lie to survive.

I've got so much living to do. Back when I was first on my own and in therapy I did so much writing. The other day, I came across one of the poems I'd written then. I almost didn't recognize it. I don't do much writing lately. Now it's more action than inaction—more real life than paper.

"

♦

M.J. is thirty-seven and has two teenaged children. "I am still finding new things to work on," she says. "I'm still finding new pieces of myself. I am trying really hard to keep in contact with the little girl inside me.

"I did find out that everybody has a little girl or boy inside them. I asked everybody I knew, people in therapy, my brothers and sister and people who have had happy childhoods. For the latter, the child is another part of their personality.

"I look at the little girl as a separate person, because I have contacted her so late. I integrate her as much as I can and sometimes I can't tell the difference between her and me. And that feels good. I am happier, calmer, not as volatile as I was before and I have fun more easily.

"It sounds strange, but the longer my father is dead, the more I like him. It's not that I forgive him really, it's just that I can see that the things he did to me and the rest of my family were because his relationship with himself was all messed up. We believed he was a monster, but monsters are created. He wasn't born like that.

"Half my family is going to Adult Children of Alcoholics (ACOA). I introduced my sister to it and my brother found it on his own. Back when I was growing up, our lives were like one big, tangled ball of string."

each small step

A.M.

Each small step
gets me closer to my destination.
Each pause and backward glance
affirms the significance
of the progress I've made
and running back to where I started
affirms my humanness,
my frailty and my constant need
to set my gaze on my destination.

Each small step
is taken with courage.
The courage to risk faltering
is the result of hard work,
pain and exhaustion.
Each doubt
reflects my insecurity
and each tear I shed
cleanses the wounds.

Each small step
cheers my heart.

bibliography

Some of these books can be found at your local library. If these titles are not available, you can ask your library to order them or to locate them via an inter-library loan. Most of the titles can be found in bookstores, particularly in women's bookstores.

Barnes, Patty D. *The Woman Inside from Incest Victim to Survivor.* Racine, Wisconsin: Mother Courage Press, 1989.

Bass, Ellen and Davis, Laura. *The Courage to Heal: A Guide for Women Survivors of Child Sexual Abuse.* New York: Harper & Row, 1988.
— A comprehensive guide for women survivors, their partners and their counsellors. Contains wide-ranging accounts and provides a complex and encouraging view of the healing process.

Bauer, Jan. *Alcoholism and Women: The Background and the Psychology.* Toronto: Inner City Books, 1982.
— This author addresses both the outer (research) and the inner (women alcoholics' experiences) aspects.

Beatie, Melody. *Codependent No More: How to Stop Controlling Others and Start Caring for Yourself.* New York: Harper & Row, 1987.
— Written by a woman counsellor and "recovered alcoholic," this book offers ideas on self-help for those who identify with the concept of "co-dependent" (someone affected by caring for an alcoholic and feeling rage, bitterness, hatred, fear, depression, helplessness, despair and guilt).

Black, Claudia. *It Will Never Happen To Me: Children of Alcoholics.* New York: Ballantine Books, 1981
— A very basic and timeless book for "adult children of alcoholics." Includes a chapter on family violence.

Black, Claudia. *Repeat After Me.* Denver, Colorado: MAC Publishing, 1985.
— A useful workbook for persons who were raised in homes in which they experienced many losses.

Blume, E. Sue. *Secret Survivors: Uncovering Incest and its Aftereffects in Women.* New York: John Wiley & Sons, 1990.

Cavington, Stephanie and Beckett, Liana. *Leaving the Enchanted Forest: The Path from Relationship Addiction to Intimacy*. San Francisco: Harper and Row, 1988.
— Clear and readable.

Danica, Elly. *Don't: A Woman's Word*. Charlottetown: gynergy books, 1988.
— *Don't: A Woman's Word* is the powerful account of Elly Danica's survival and healing. As a child, she was brutally abused by her father and the men he "gave" her to. The voices of the child she once was, the woman she used to be and the woman she is now speak in numbered journal-like entries. Danica explores various gateways— entrances into memory and her body.

Davis, Laura. *The Courage to Heal Workbook*. New York: Harper and Row, 1990.
— Many people have found the exercises in this workbook very relevant.

Evert, Kathy and Bijerk, Inie. *When You're Ready: A Woman's Healing from Childhood Physical and Sexual Abuse by her Mother*. Walnut Creek: Launch Press, 1987.
— Kathy Evert and her therapist describe the process by which Kathy reclaimed the secret world of her child self—a world that included physical abuse and pre-verbal sexual abuse by her mother. Of aboriginal background, Kathy depicts every aspect of her experience. Inie Bijeck describes her response to working with Kathy and offers valuable advice to others.

Forward, Susan. *Toxic Parents*. New York: Bantam Books, 1989.

Fraser, Sylvia. *My Father's House*. Toronto: Doubleday Canada Limited, 1987.
— Very readable and gives a clear sense of dissociation.

Friends in Recovery. *The 12 Steps for Adult Children From Addictive and Other Dysfunctional Families*. San Diego: Recovery Publications, Inc., 1989.
— This book focuses on Alcoholics' Anonymous 12 Step Program as it applies to children who grew up in a dysfunctional environment due to their parents' alcoholism.

Gil, Eliana M. Ph. D. *Outgrowing the Pain*. New York: Dell Publishing, 1983.

Hryniuk, Angela. *Walking Inside Circles*. Charlottetown: gynergy books, 1989.

Laulan, JoAnn. *Lesbian Passion*. San Francisco: Spinsters/Aunt Lute, 1987.
— Clear, easy to read, written with a lot of humour and very insightful. This book is useful for *all* women.

Lerner, Harriet Goldhor. *The Dance of Anger*. New York: Harper and Row, 1988.

Maltz, Wendy and Holman, Beverly. *Incest and Sexuality: A Guide to Understanding and Healing.* Toronto: Lexington Books, 1987.
— An affirming book for adult survivors, their partners and therapists. The authors address concerns and difficulties surrounding adult sexuality in terms of how these are rooted in childhood sexual abuse. Their emphasis is on validation, communication and support; and they offer a practical guide to reclaiming a positive sense of sexuality.

McDaniel, Judith. *Metamorphosis: Reflections on Recovery.* New York: Firebrand Books, 1989.
— Through prose and poetry, writer and political activist McDaniel engagingly shares her personal interpretation of the Alcoholics Anonymous 12 Step Program from a feminist perspective.

Rush, Florence. *The Best Kept Secret: Sexual Abuse of Children.* New York: McGraw-Hill, 1980.

Sandmaier, Marion. *The Invisible Alcoholics: Women and Alcohol Abuse in America.* New York: McGraw-Hill, 1980.

Sisk, Shiela L. and Hoffman, Charlotte Foster. *Inside Scars: Incest Recovery as Told by a Survivor and Her Therapist.* Gainsville: Pandora Press, 1987.

Swallow, Jean, ed. *Out from Under: Sober Dykes and Our Friends.* San Francisco: Spinsters/Aunt Lute, 1983.

Utain, Marsha and Oliver, Barbara. *Scream Louder, Through Hell and Healing with an Incest Survivor and her Therapist.* Florida: Health Communications, Inc., 1989.

Wisechild, Louise. *The Obsidian Mirror: an Adult Healing From Incest.* Seattle: Seal Press, 1988.

The Women's Research Centre. *Recollecting Our Lives: Women's Experience of Childhood Sexual Abuse.* Vancouver: Press Gang Pub., 1989

NEW AND RECENT RELEASES FROM GYNERGY BOOKS

- **By Word of Mouth: Lesbians write the erotic,** *Lee Fleming (ed.).* A bedside book of short fiction and poetry by thirty-one lesbian writers from Canada and the United States. $ 10.95

- **Don't: A Woman's Word,** *Elly Danica.* The best-selling account of incest and recovery, both horrifying and hauntingly beautiful in its eventual triumph over the past. $ 8.95

- **Double Negative,** *Daphne Marlatt* and *Betsy Warland.* An innovative collaboration that redefines boundaries and images of women from a lesbian feminist perspective. $ 8.95 / $ 7.95 US

- **Each Small Step: Breaking the chains of abuse and addiction,** *Marilyn MacKinnon (ed.).* This groundbreaking anthology contains personal narratives by women at various stages of recovery from the traumas of childhood sexual abuse and alcohol and chemical dependency. $ 10.95

- **Fascination and other bar stories,** *Jackie Manthorne.* These are satisfying stories of the rituals of seduction and sexuality in the otherworld of lesbian bars—fascinating fiction for lesbians. $ 9.95

- **getting wise,** *Marg Yeo.* Women-loving poems of resistance and triumph. Marg Yeo shares hard-won truths and "the fine delight there will always be for me in poems and women." $ 8.95 / $ 7.95 US

- **The Montreal Massacre,** *Marie Chalouh* and *Louise Malette (eds.).* Feminist letters, essays and poems examine the mass murder of fourteen women at Ecole Polytechnique in Montreal, Quebec on December 6, 1989. The writers express a common theme: the massacre was the extreme manifestation of misogyny in our patriarchal society. $ 12.95

- **Somebody Should Kiss You,** *Brenda Brooks.* An intimate, humorous and bold collection of poetry that celebrate the courage of lesbian lives and loves. $ 8.95 / $ 7.95 US

- **Tide Lines: Stories of change by lesbians,** *Lee Fleming (ed.).* These diverse stories explore the many faces of change—instantaneous, over-a-lifetime, subtle or cataclysmic. $ 10.95

gynergy books is distributed in Canada by UTP, in the U.S. by Bookpeople and Inland and in the U.K. by Turnaround. Individual orders can be sent, prepaid, to: *gynergy books*, P.O. Box 2023, Charlottetown, PEI, Canada, C1A 7N7. Please add postage and handling ($1.50 for the first book and 75 cents for each additional book) to your order. Canadian residents add 7% GST to the total amount. GST registration number R104383120.